William McKinley and Our America
A Pictorial History

Good reading &
All Best Wishes -
Enjoy my book!

Psalm 139

William McKinley and Our America

A Pictorial History

by Richard L. McElroy

Stark County Historical Society
Canton, Ohio
1996

This book is dedicated to my father and mother, Lee and Virginia McElroy of Carrollton, Ohio; and to the memory of Henry S. Belden, III of Canton who, along with his family, helped to preserve the historical heritage of the McKinleys.

✂ CONTENTS ✂

⨯ ACKNOWLEDGEMENTS ⨯

This project began in 1988 and initially took me to numerous Ohio communities including Niles, East Liverpool, Youngstown, Fremont, Poland, Lisbon, Navarre, Minerva, Cleveland and Columbus. In addition, I visited Somerset, Pennsylvania, the battlefields of Antietam and South Mountain in Maryland, Washington, D.C., Arlington, Virginia, and Key West, Florida (the latter two having memorials to the battleship Maine and graves of sailors killed in the explosion aboard that ship in 1898).

Jim Strawn and Jim Ewing, board members of the Stark County Historical Society, examined my manuscript and suggested the Society (which operates the McKinley Museum) underwrite the publishing. Through their contacts I met Bill Wyss, former curator/historian of the McKinley Museum in Canton. Bill gave me complete access and use of all photos and documents. He also read the book and offered valuable input. Librarian Bud Weber also took time to authenticate McKinley-related material.

A host of others at the McKinley Museum were helpful. Among these were Rosemary Anderson, Eileen Babik, Sally Donze, Jo Wilson, DeFrance Thomas, Janet Whitacre, Jean Griffin, Rita Zwick, Jean Roth, and Liz Hillick. Nan Johnston, who also serves as Director of the Stark County District Library, coordinated efforts to publish and publicize the book. Member Karl Harsh, one of the best authorities on local history, gave added attention to detail. Jennifer Thompson, whose creative talents brought the pictures to life, did the layout of more than 500 photographs and captions. Betty Elsaesser carefully scrutinized the manuscript and improved its structure. Ward J. Timken and the Timken Foundation gave their wholehearted support in helping to finance this undertaking. The families of Henry S. Belden III and Marshall Belden, both active members in the Stark County Historical Society, provided direction.

Others living in the greater Canton area supplied information and photographs. These included: Tom Hayes, Mary Regula, Reverend Douglas Patton, Paul Keller, Carol Neiss, Angela Smith, Ray Bules, John Arnold, Ralph Thompson, Sue Farley, Sally Efremoff, Amy Shriver, Patricia Locke, Richard and Katherine Babik, Reverend Bruce Boak, Stewart Witham, Larry Moesle, Jamie Paquette, church secretaries Virginia Gingrich and Marge Morris, artists Emmett Boyd and Nikhil Patel, Dennis Grady and David McCauley of Grady-McCauley, Inc., Howard Ripple of the William McKinley Masonic Lodge, and Hoover Historical Center personnel Stacey Krammes, Ann Haines, and Ruth Basner. Writers Gary Brown and Mark Price of the Canton *Repository* and Mary Cain and Dan Mucci of the Canton *Free Press* were also sources of information.

While conducting research at various institutions I had the good fortune of assistance from many individuals. These people were Roger Bridges, Becky Hill and Gil Gonzalez at the Rutherford B. Hayes Presidential Library in Fremont, Ohio; Margaret Moser at the Pelletier Library at Allegheny College, Meadville, Pennsylvania; Ann Yancura of the National McKinley Birthplace Memorial in Niles, Ohio; Yvonne Murchinson-Foote at the Buffalo and Erie County Historical Society in New York; Nadine Sturdy of the public library in Bellaire, Michigan; Rev. Richard Powell also of Bellaire; photographer Dick Griffin of Carrollton, Ohio; Columbus residents Vernon Pack, Joanne Rainey, and Tom and Linda Robbins; Burl and Esther Adams, and Jim and Joyce Falconer (along with their children), all of whom live on the property which was once the McKinley farm in Minerva, Ohio; Youngstown City Hall employees Mary Catherine Sanders, Ann Tokarsky, Roger Linker and Ray Novak; Pamela Pletcher, archivist at the Mahoning Valley (Ohio) Historical Society; Gayle Ridge, Barb Heck, Patti Sidell, and Elizabeth Thompson of Poland, Ohio; Marilyn Droney of Youngstown; library employees Mark Guyer and Mary Carey of Canton; State Senator Scott Oelslager of Canton (who located several photos); and professor Tom Sosnowski of Kent State University who lives in North Canton.

Library of Congress personnel Mary Ison, Jane Van Nimmen, and Jennifer Brathovde helped find and identify scores of McKinley pictures. While in Washington I also met photographer Rudy Vetter of Alexandria, Virginia, and his friend George Hobart of nearby Arlington. A former curator of the photography division at the Library of Congress, George shed some new light on my research. He is a direct descendant of McKinley's vice-president, Garret Hobart.

Sallie Chatfield of College Park, Maryland, was extremely helpful at The National Archives, as were Cathy Bogus and Don Singer who also work there. Greg and Joanne Hamilton of Rockville, Maryland, served as guides and provided input during my stays in the nation's capital. Betty Monkman of the White House lent aid in locating some photos as well.

U.S. Congressman Ralph Regula, an authority on McKinley, and his able administrative assistant Daryl Revoldt, made arrangements for my research in Washington. Daryl also read the manuscript and offered useful advice which improved its context. Regula's former aide, Bob Gorman, gave some input as well.

My sources were many and varied. One was the *McKinley Papers,* more then one hundred volumes, all available on microfilm. Hundreds of other manuscripts and boxes of memorabilia offered rich information. Old records such as birth certificates, genealogies, court papers and newspaper clippings proved valuable. I also interviewed many people who either owned McKinley-related material or were related to the McKinley family.

The National Archives contains two unique collections of photographs — those of Adolphus Greely and D.L. Brainard. The Brainard Collection spanned a period from the 1870s to the 1920s. As an Army Signal Corps officer, Brainard traveled extensively throughout the nation and abroad. Another source was the Frances Benjamin Johnston Collection at the Library of Congress. A pioneer in photography, she worked at the White House during the Cleveland and McKinley administrations as an official photographer, and often accompanied the McKinleys on trips away from Washington.

I owe a debt of gratitude to editor Mike Hanke of the Canton *Repository.* For more than a year Mike allowed me to study and reshoot two hundred McKinley photographs and articles. My wife Pamela spent hours helping me organize these photos. The "lion's share" of my pictures, however, came from the McKinley Museum in Canton. Without the cooperation of the museum staff and concerned members of the Stark County Historical Society, this book would not have been possible.

During the course of my work I examined well over ten thousand illustrations and photographs. Approximately five hundred of these were reproduced by Canton photographer Tim Wedekamm. Director of Media Services at Aultman Hospital in Canton, Tim also runs his own photography business. He was less than honest with me when he initially warned, "I can't make a copy of a picture better than the original." Tim was able to take old photographs and daguerreotypes, many of them in poor condition, and reproduce pictures to a near state of perfection. Over a span of eighteen months his efforts begat illustrations which were clear and appealing to the eye. Liz Krammes consulted on the format to compliment the history of William McKinley.

Last, and by no means least, is Joyce Yut of the McKinley Museum in Canton. As an active member and trustee of the Stark County Historical Society and director of the McKinley Museum, she took a special interest in this project. Armed with her portable laptop computer, she spent hours on end typing the manuscript. Her diligence, patience, enthusiasm, meticulous care, constructive criticism, and attention to detail turned a rough-hewn collection of typed pages and pictures into a much-improved work. It is no exaggeration in saying that without her guiding hand this book would have been an impossibility.

The kindness, trust, concern and consideration all of these people demonstrated convinced me that we all share a common bond—preserving the heritage of our nation's twenty-fifth president. In reading this book, my fellow Americans may gain a fresh look and better understanding of the contributions and achievements of this kindly gentleman from Ohio. ▩

∽INTRODUCTION∾

The life of William McKinley spanned the last half of the nineteenth century. Born of humble origin, he briefly attended college, taught school and clerked in a post office. He then volunteered to fight in the Civil War where he served with distinction. Trained as a lawyer during the post-war period, he devoted his career to politics. He served as a county prosecutor, congressman, governor and president.

McKinley witnessed the accelerating changes of America, from essentially a rural nation to an industrial world power.

In the pages which follow, Rich McElroy's text and unique collection of photographs document the changing world of William McKinley. Although the photographs cannot completely capture McKinley's personality, character or mannerisms, they help provide a detailed insightful glimpse of the man and his times.

McKinley was known as a man with a steadfast belief in God, country and family. He was intelligent and modest enough to adapt his world view when developments called for a change. Once a well-known proponent of tariffs, he supported increased free trade as the industrial capacity of the United States grew and foreign markets became attractive. As president, McKinley proclaimed, "The period of exclusiveness is past. The expansion of our trade and commerce is the pressing problem."

McKinley's devotion to his wife, Ida, and his compassion for even his enemies are evident from the events surrounding his assassination. His first words expressed after he was shot were for the safety of his assassin who was being manhandled in a scuffle with onlookers. He next cautioned his staff to be careful how they informed Ida of the shooting.

In his Memorial Address to Congress in 1902, Secretary of State John Hay observed that McKinley's words and deeds "were all the instinctive expressions of a nature so lofty and pure that pride in its nobility at once softened and enhanced the Nation's sense of loss." Hay concluded his address by saying that every American "must feel his devotion for his country renewed and kindled when he remembers how McKinley loved, revered and served..."

William McKinley's vision for government may be summed up in his words from a speech on human rights: "The foundation of our government is liberty; its superstructure peace."

McKinley lived—and died—as a gentle but strong force for the ideals of freedom and peace.

Ralph Regula, United States House of Representatives

↬ QUOTATIONS ↫
by William McKinley

Duty determines destiny.

A man's best gift to his country is his life's blood.

Pride and power must not taint motives.

Reduce the tariff and laborers are the first to suffer.

Our differences are policies, our agreements principles.

Expositions are the timekeepers of progress.

Regular employment, good wages, and education bring prosperity and happiness.

I have to think when I speak!

We have no time to waste in this short, hurrying life.

God and man have linked the nations together.

The virtue that comes out from the holy altar of the home is the most priceless gift this nation has.

I trust we may always preserve the purity of our American homes. From this comes good citizenship.

A religious spirit helps every man.

Our country with its great institutions is safe so long as virtue resides in the home and patriotism abides in the hearts of the people.

Our flag has never waved over any community but in blessing.

Men and women are books, and events are life's vast volume of illustrations.

An open schoolhouse, free to all, evidences the highest type of advanced civilization.

Four hundred thousand teachers and fifteen million pupils are a pillar of strength to our government.

Luck will not last. It may help you once, but you cannot count on it.

Labor is the only key to opportunity.

Make it possible to break down the prejudice of the past. Get out from under your ancestral tree.

Let us ever remember that our interest is in Concord, not Conflict [sic], and that our real eminence rests in the victories of peace, not those of war.

Legislation helpful to producers is beneficial to all.

American workmen are, as a body, the most ingenious and intelligent of the world.

Self preservation is the first law of nature, as it is and should be of nations.

Unlike any other nation, here the people rule. Their law is supreme.

I have never been in doubt since I was old enough to think intelligently that I would someday be made president of the United States.

Exact knowledge is the requirement of the hour; you will be crippled without it.

Half-heartedness never won a battle.

A cause which is right is never lost.

My rule is to make haste slowly.

We cannot always do what is best, but we can do what is practical at the time.

Every mother wants her son to become president, but no mother wants her son to become a politician.

One thing essential to getting on in the world is to have a purpose. Life without it will prove a failure, and all your efforts barren of results.

I shall never get into a war until I am sure that God and man approve.

I would rather have my political economy founded upon the everyday experience of the puddler or the potter than the learning of the professor.

Good money never made hard times.

We may differ in our political and religious beliefs, but we are united for country.

Loyalty to the government is our national creed.

Side by side with education must be character.

Nothing in the world is worth so much, will last so long, and serve its possessor so well as good character.

A religious spirit helps every man.

Legislation helpful to producers is beneficial to all.

In the darkest hours of defeat victory may be near.

With patriotism in our hearts and with the flag of our country in the hands of our children there is no danger of anarchy and there will be no danger to the Union.

ILLUSTRATED TIMELINE
Of William McKinley's life

1 8 4 0 ' s – 1 8 5 0 ' s

Birthplace in Niles, Ohio

1843 Born January 29 in Niles, Ohio

1846 Baby sister "Abbie" died

1849 Entered the district school in Niles

1852 Moved to nearby Poland

1859 Joined the Methodist Church

Main Street Poland, Ohio

1 8 6 0 ' s

McKinley as a youth

1860 Briefly attended Allegheny College in Meadville, Pennsylvania; taught school for a winter term in Poland after leaving college

1861 Worked as a clerk in Poland Post Office; joined the Twenty-third Ohio Volunteer Infantry at beginning of Civil War

1863 Clashed with Morgan's Raiders at Buffington Island, Ohio

1864 Fought at Cloyd's Mountain and Winchester, Virginia; promoted to captain

Allegheny College in Meadville

1 8 6 0 ' s

The young officer McKinley

1865 Promoted to major by brevet; discharged from army after war ended

1866 Attended Albany, New York, Law School

1867 Admitted to the Ohio Bar; moved to Canton

1868 Sister Mary died; elected president of Canton Y.M.C.A.

1869 Elected Stark County prosecutor

As a student at law school

ILLUSTRATED TIMELINE

Of William McKinley's life

---

1 8 7 0 ' s

Newlyweds William and Ida McKinley

1871 Married Ida Saxton January 25; daugher Katie born December 25

1873 Baby Ida died four months and twenty-two days after birth; Mrs. McKinley became ill; brother Abner became a law partner; James Saxton appointed McKinley as bank manager

1875 Daughter Katie succumbed to heart failure; returned to Congress after having been defeated in 1871 re-election bid for prosecutor

Daughter Katie

---

1 8 7 0 ' s

McKinley as a U.S. Congressman

1876 Elected to United States House of Representatives, served 1877-84, 1885-91; later became chairman of House Ways and Means Committee

Sketch of McKinley as Congressman

---

1 8 8 0 ' s

Nephew James F. McKinley

1884 Lost his seat in Congress as a result of a dispute over 1882 election results; returned to Congress in fall election; with industrialist Cornelius Aultman he established the Canton Public Library

1889 Brother James died; his two children, Grace and James were brought to live in the McKinley household in Canton

McKinley home in Canton

ILLUSTRATED TIMELINE

Of William McKinley's life

---

1 8 9 0 ' s

Ohio's thirty-ninth governor

1890 McKinley Tariff Act adopted; defeated for Congress by John Warwick of Massilion; Sister Anna, long-time Canton teacher, died

1891 Elected governor of Ohio and served two two-year terms

1892 Brother David, former United States Minister to Hawaii, died; father William died at age eighty-five.

Mark Hanna

---

1 8 9 0 ' s

1893 Dedicated the Ohio Building at the Chicago World's Fair; re-elected governor; faced financial ruin; Mark Hanna became McKinley's presidential campaign manager.

1896 Moved back to Canton into the North Market Street home where they had previously lived; nominated for president in June; elected in November

McKinley's Mother

1897 Inaugurated March 4 as twenty-fifth president; mother Nancy died at age eighty-eight

1898 Signed declaration of war against Spain on April 20

1899 Philippine Insurrection

---

1 9 0 0 ' s

McKinley assassination

1900 Boxer Rebellion in China; re-elected president

1901 Shot at Pan American Exposition in Buffalo on September 6; died at 2:15 A.M. on September 14

1904 Brother Abner died

1907 Wife Ida died at age fifty-nine; McKinley National Memorial dedicated in Canton September 30

McKinley Memorial Canton, Ohio

"Therefore I summon age to grant youth's heritage."
–Robert Browning

CHAPTER I

A HERITAGE AND A BOYHOOD

The ancestors of our twenty-fifth president came from Scotland and northern Ireland. In the 1540s, these people took the name of MacIanla, or sons of I-on-lay. One branch of the family lived in Scotland in the middle and late 1600s, and one James McKinlay became well known for his bravery in battle. His clan adopted a crest of an armed man holding an olive branch and the motto "Not too much." Several years later, some descendants of this family moved to Ulster County in northern Ireland.

The president's great-great-great grandfather, David McKinley, was the first of the family to emigrate to America. In 1743, he settled in Chanceford Township, Pennsylvania, near the Maryland border, purchasing three hundred sixteen acres of land overlooking the Susquehanna River. He and his wife, Esther, had three sons and a daughter. A weaver and farmer, David was elected township supervisor in 1750. He died seven years later.

David's oldest son, John, born in 1728, was McKinley's great-great grandfather. John and his wife Margaret had eight children. He served in the militia during the American Revolution and later worked a number of jobs — farmer, blacksmith, weaver, whiskey distiller, and transporter. He owned

This farmstead was the ancestral home of William McKinley. It was located at Conagher, near Ballmoney in northern Ireland. (Stark County Historical Society)

Close-up of the same home in Antrim County, northern Ireland. (*Collier's* magazine.)

W. McKinley

(right) Interior view of ancestral Irish home. (Timken Company)

(below) McKinley's other ancestors came from central Scotland. Here is the MacKinley clan tombstone at St. Bride's Cemetery near Edinburgh, Scotland. (Stark County Historical Society)

(above) Another view of the cemetery at St. Bride's Chapel. (Stark County Historical Society)

(right) The Homestead Tract farm of McKinley's ancestors in Chanceford Township, York County, Pennsylvania. (Stark County Historical Society)

Farmhouse of the Chanceford Township property. (Hoover Company)

Grandfather James S. McKinley, who lived in New Lisbon, Ohio. After operating the Rebecca Iron Furnace, he moved to Indiana, settling near South Bend. (Stark County Historical Society)

many horses and wagons in Pennsylvania and Maryland. John died in York County, Pennsylvania, on February 18, 1779. His oldest child, David, was McKinley's great grandfather.

David was born on May 16, 1755. As an eleven year old, he joined the local militia in Chanceford Township. His group of fifty-nine men became part of the sixth company of York County's Sixth Battalion. Thus, both he and his father served in the war. Until 1779 the Sixth Battalion served under the direct command of George Washington in the Continental Army. David participated in the Battles of Amboy, Chestnut Hill, and Paulus Hook. He married Sarah Gray and they moved to Mercer County, Pennsylvania, about twenty-five miles northeast of Youngstown, Ohio. David and Sarah had four sons and six daughters. After thirty-four years of marriage, Sarah died.

David remarried on September 1, 1815, taking Eleanor McClane as his wife. He and Eleanor settled in New Lisbon (Lisbon) in Columbiana County, Ohio, where they remained for the next twenty years. David farmed and taught school, and when Eleanor died in 1835, he moved in with his son James, a wealthy farmer and ironmaker in Columbiana County, Ohio. David McKinley died on August 8, 1840.

James McKinley, the president's grandfather, married Mary Rose. They lived in Lisbon in an old sandstone house built by Gideon Hughes, operator of the nearby Rebecca Iron Furnace. Mary's father, Andrew Rose (McKinley's other great grandfather), fought in the Continental Army, later leaving to manufacture cannons and bullets for the American cause. James and Mary had thirteen children, includ-

(Charles Sumner Van Tassel)

(Stark County Historical Society)

Three views on this page of the Rebecca Blast Furnace, years after its destruction. Built by Gideon Hughes, it was the first iron furnace built west of the Allegheny Mountains and was later operated by William McKinley, Sr. in the late 1830s. The top picture was taken in the 1890s; and the other two in the 1920s. (Stark County Historical Society)

(Stark County Historical Society)

Schoolhouse in Lisbon where David McKinley, William's great-grandfather, taught. (Stark County Historical Society)

(Charles Sumner Van Tassel)   (Stark County Historical Society)

Three pictures of the William McKinley, Sr. home, built and owned by Gideon Hughes near Lisbon, Ohio. Picture above left was taken in the 1880s. William McKinley, Sr. and his wife Nancy Allison moved from here before their son William was born. Later, the building became a headquarters for the Boy Scouts of Columbiana County.

(Stark County Historical Society)

ing son William (McKinley's father), born on November 15, 1807.

During the War of 1812 James fought under the command of General William Henry Harrison. James and Mary later moved to western Ohio in Crawford County, probably in 1836. Characteristic of the adventurous, restless spirit of his Scottish-Irish ancestors, James moved again at age fifty-nine. He and Mary settled in Warren Township near present-day South Bend, Indiana. They both died on the same day, August 20, 1847. Ironically, this was their anniversary. It is believed their deaths resulted from food poisoning after a dinner given in their honor. James was nearly sixty-four years old and Mary was fifty-nine.

William McKinley, Sr. and Nancy Allison met each other at the Methodist church in Lisbon. They were married on June 6, 1829. Soon thereafter they moved several miles north where William sought to establish himself as an iron maker. William and Nancy had nine children, four sons and five daughters.

Not much is documented about Nancy Allison McKinley's ancestors. We do know that the Allisons were among the early founders of Donegal Church in northern Ireland. John Allison married Jean Brownlee; their son Gavin was Nancy's grandfather. The family settled in Virginia, probably in the 1730s. The Allisons then moved to Pennsylvania where Gavin's son, Abner Allison (maternal grandfather of the president), grew up. Abner married Ann Campbell and, following the Great Indian Trail, moved to Columbiana County, Ohio, near Lisbon. During the War of 1812, Abner served under William Henry Harrison, and it is likely that both of William McKinley's grandfathers knew each other while fighting in that conflict. In 1809 Abner and Ann's daughter Nancy was born.

The twenty-fifth president of the United States was the seventh of nine children born to William and Nancy McKinley. A brief summary of McKinley's siblings is as follows:

<u>David McKinley</u>, born in 1829, died on September 18, 1892; moved to California in 1856; served as United States Consul to Hawaii from 1881-85; lived several years in San Francisco and Honolulu; died in Pennsylvania.

<u>Anna McKinley</u>, born in 1832, died July 29, 1890; was a teacher and principal for many years in Canton, Ohio; died at age fifty-eight.

<u>James McKinley</u>, born in 1834, died October 12, 1889; lived for several years in California and died of a stroke in New Castle, Pennsylvania; he and his wife had three children: Hope, Grace, and James F.

<u>Mary McKinley May</u>, born in 1835; lived in Poland, Ohio, where she passed away June 28, 1868, at age thirty-two.

<u>Helen McKinley</u>, born in 1837, died June 9, 1924; also taught school in Canton, and later in Cleveland, where she died at age eighty-seven.

<u>Sarah McKinley Duncan</u>, born in 1840, died November 22, 1931; married Andrew Jackson Duncan; a former schoolteacher, she lived in Cleveland, Ohio, until her death at age ninety-one.

William McKinley, Sr., like his father, operated several blast furnaces. He and his wife were strict Methodists and lived near the city of Youngstown, Ohio. (Canton *Repository*)

Nancy Allison McKinley, one of nine children, was raised in Lisbon. Her ancestors also came from Scotland. (Stark County Historical Society)

As a child, William McKinley did not have any pets. But as president he was the proud owner of a parrot he named Washington Post. He taught it to whistle "Yankee Doodle."

<u>Abigail McKinley</u>, born in 1845 (after William); died in infancy on January 26, 1846.

<u>Abner McKinley</u>, born 1847, died June 11, 1904; became a lawyer and served briefly as a partner with his brother William in Canton; in 1888 he moved to New York City, and later to Somerset, Pennsylvania; he and his wife Annie had a daughter Mabel; Abner's death was due to Bright's Disease.

William McKinley, Jr. was born in Niles, Ohio, on January 29, 1843. The family lived on the upper floor of a two-story frame house with a country store downstairs and located on a corner of the main street, .

During the Mexican War, the five-year-old boy, along with playmates, dressed up and drilled like American soldiers. When William was nine years old, the family moved to nearby Poland, Ohio.

As a child, Will (as he was called) played with his older sisters Anna and Helen. He became proficient with the bow and arrow, marbles, ice skating, and kite flying. He also enjoyed fishing in Mosquito Creek, though he grew to dislike this activity in later years.

One of William McKinley's fondest and most cherished memories was when he was a boy in Niles, Ohio, and had to gather in the milk cows each morning. In his bare feet, even during winter, he hurried over the ground, stopping periodically to warm them where the cows had lain. He also developed a love for animals and could not stand to see them suffer.

William McKinley's birthplace in Niles, Ohio. A general store was located down below, in the left of the photo. The house was later moved and in 1937 was destroyed by a fire. A bank building is presently at the site. (Canton *Repository*)

(right)This black iron kettle, used by the McKinley family, was made by the President's grandfather, James Stevenson McKinley, at his Lisbon foundry. (National McKinley Birthplace Memorial)

(far right)Both of the spinning wheels pictured here were used by the McKinley family. (National McKinley Birthplace Memorial)

Another picture of the president's mother. (Stark County Historical Society)

McKinley's Poland home as it looked in the 1890s. The building was torn down more than a century ago. (N.G. Hamilton Publishing Company)

Maria Kryle, McKinley's first teacher. She died in 1918. (McKinley National Birthplace Memorial)

The Poland Seminary where McKinley attended school. This photograph was taken five days before the collapse of the building, which occurred on November 23, 1895. A new building was erected on the same foundation. Today, this site is the location of Poland Middle School at 47 College Street. (N.G. Hamilton Publishing Company)

Main Street in Poland, Ohio, as it appeared in 1895. The building at the extreme left is the village post office where McKinley was a clerk. (N.G. Hamilton Publishing Company)

Even at an early age, McKinley demonstrated his patience and determination when he went fishing with several other boys. After a couple of hours, his friends decided to go swimming since they had caught no fish. McKinley insisted on staying, and while the other boys frolicked downstream, he fished for several hours and took home an impressive catch.

The McKinley household encouraged learning and discussion. After dinner the children were required to read, or be read to. McKinley particularly recalled books by Dickens, the works of Shakespeare, as well as abolitionist newspapers and the *Bible*. Among his favorite novels were *Robinson Crusoe* and *Swiss Family Robinson*.

Though not particularly fond of school, he was studious. He worked hard to get high marks. A boyhood friend revealed that McKinley "reached his conclusions almost by intuition." Indeed, his real education came not from books, but from keen observation. He possessed common sense and studied long hours to please his mother and sisters. Two teachers, B.F. Lee and Miss E.M. Blakeless, inspired him at the Poland Seminary.

McKinley's father built and operated several iron furnaces, like his father before him. William, Sr. made little money in this business, however, and his frequent absences from home left the task of raising the younger children to his wife and older daughters.

Anna McKinley never married. She taught school and served as a principal in Canton. McKinley High School was named after both her and William. (Stark County Historical Society)

When President McKinley was seventeen, his parents sent him to a Methodist institution, Allegheny College in Meadville, Pennsylvania. An incident which occurred while he was at the college in 1860 left an impression on his fellow students. One of McKinley's southern classmates proposed a toast to Confederate leader Jefferson Davis. McKinley refused to drink, declaring he would rather fight on southern soil than accept treason. He attended the college only a short time when he became ill. He returned home, not only physically and mentally exhausted but lacking funds as well. With family finances severely limited following the Panic of 1857, he decided to go to work.

Raised in a strict Methodist home, McKinley learned the value of education. He accepted an appointment to teach in a one room schoolhouse in the Kerr District School, about three miles from his home. There he worked for a term, being paid twenty-five dollars a month. He then became Poland's assistant postmaster in early 1861.

With Abraham Lincoln's election and subsequent inauguration, eleven southern states seceded from the Union. When Fort Sumter was fired on by Confederate forces in April of 1861, Lincoln called for seventy-five thousand volunteers. The men of Poland responded quickly by joining the army, but McKinley was not one of them. As he often demonstrated, he did not make an important decision until he had consulted his parents and sought the advice of friends. ▨

McKinley's sister, Helen, also taught school in Canton, and was a noted singer. (Stark County Historical Society)

Abner McKinley, prominent attorney, worked as a law partner with his brother William. (Stark County Historical Society)

Former Poland classmates of McKinley. (McKinley National Birthplace Memorial)

CHAPTER II

THE YOUTH BECOMES A MAN

The 1861 contingent of Poland Guards was made up of hometown boys and men who figured that they would be serving in the army for only three months. Instead it became three years. McKinley did not volunteer rashly, characteristic of a man who rarely did anything on impulse.

Both he and his cousin, Will Osborne, watched their friends leave for Camp Chase in Columbus, Ohio. As a young man of eighteen, McKinley carefully deliberated about what he should do. He asked his mother what she thought, and she told him, "I think you ought to go." McKinley and Will enlisted, reported to Camp Chase a couple of days later, and were assigned to Company E of the Twenty-third Ohio Volunteer Infantry. McKinley was sworn into service on July 11, 1861, by General John C. Fremont, "The Pathfinder." Years later, McKinley recalled this moment: "I remember he pounded my chest and looked square into my eyes and finally pronounced me fit for a soldier."

Old rifles which had been made during the War of 1812 were issued to McKinley's unit. Many recruits protested, some to the point of mutiny. The unit's commander, future president Rutherford B. Hayes, talked with McKinley and, together, they convinced the men of the Ohio twenty-third to wait until

As a student at the Poland Academy, McKinley was diligent, rather than clever. Sincere and sensitive, he preferred debate to other activities. He got along well with the other students and was submissive to the pious dictates of his mother. (Stark County Historical Society)

Bentley Hall, the main building on the campus of Allegheny College in Meadville, Pennsylvania. McKinley attended classes for a term until a combination of ill health and poor finances forced him to leave. Nearly thirty-five years later he returned as the governor of Ohio to give the commencement address and receive an honorary Doctorate of Law degree. (Allegheny College)

William McKinley, Jr. at age sixteen in 1859. (Stark County Historical Society)

The present Odd Fellows Home in Meadville. After traveling by stagecoach from Youngstown, McKinley and his cousin Will Osborne lived here while attending college. In 1859, the home was a boardinghouse kept by Dr. Goe. The McKinley Room is preserved with appropriate portraits. (Allegheny College)

The schoolhouse near Poland where McKinley taught school. The building was torn down many years ago. (N.G. Hamilton Publishing Company)

Illustration of McKinley as a teacher in the Kerr District School near Poland, Ohio. *(Judge* magazine*)*

(far left) The post office in Poland where McKinley worked after teaching school. (Charles Olcott)

(left) The old Sparrow Tavern in Poland. Built in 1804, it was in this building that McKinley enlisted as a Union soldier. (Church of The Savior United Methodist of Canton)

Two ambrotypes of Camp Chase in 1861. It was here that McKinley and his cousin Will Osborne reported for duty. (Ohio Historical Society)

better rifles arrived. Thus, a possible revolt was avoided even though the camp was marked by numerous problems of discipline, sanitation, and improper equipment.

McKinley's first taste of warfare came after pursuing Confederate guerrilla fighters in the western counties of Virginia. He wrote in his diary, "It may be that I will never see the light of another day. Should this be my fate, I fall in a good cause and hope to fall in the arms of my Blessed Redeemer." After serving as a private and cook for nearly eleven months, he was appointed commissary sergeant in April of 1862. As he oversaw the food supply and rations, McKinley may have believed he would see little combat. The battlefield soon changed this idea and tested his bravery.

In the summer of 1862 Confederate General Robert E. Lee and 40,000 troops invaded Maryland. The rebels needed the rich storehouses of food and supplies there. For four days in September, Union Generals George McClellan and Joseph Hooker, with a force of 87,000 men, tried to check Lee's advance. At the battles of South Mountain and Antietam, McKinley became more than a mere spectator. He saw his commander, Colonel Hayes, severely wounded at South Mountain. Then, two days later on September 17, the armies fought again at Antietam Creek near Sharpsburg.

More men were killed on this single day than in any battle in the western hemisphere. The total number of casualties exceeded twenty-three thousand. McKinley's regiment, the Ohio Twenty-third, lost two hundred men (half of its

William McKinley, age eighteen, at the beginning of the Civil War. (Canton *Repository*)

McKinley's Civil War rifle. (Canton *Repository*)

The young officer McKinley worked in the commissary unit preparing and distributing food. (Canton *Repository*)

McKinley in a Napoleonic pose. (Stark County Historical Society)

McKinley sported a beard and mustache to give him an older look. (Stark County Historical Society)

McKinley's immediate commanding officer was Colonel Rutherford B. Hayes (later Ohio governor and the nineteenth United States president). Hayes regarded McKinley as a younger brother. McKinley said of Hayes, "His whole nature seemed to change when in battle. From the sunny, agreeable, the kind, the generous, the gentle gentleman.....he was, when the battle was once on....intense and ferocious." (Library of Congress)

In this lithograph two Ohio regiments capture a stone rail and fence at Turner's Gap near South Mountain, Maryland, on September 15, 1862. Lieutenant Colonel Hayes was severely wounded. He is shown at the left above the two wagons. It was here that McKinley got his "baptism of fire," seeing the war close up while working as a quartermaster. (Library of Congress)

Hayes and McKinley spent part of the winter of 1861-62 in these cottages in Beckley (formerly Raleigh), West Virginia. Lucy Hayes visited her husband and mothered McKinley, describing him as a "happy jolly boy of twenty." She wrote that McKinley spent so much time tending the main camp fires that she nicknamed him "Casabiana." The nickname fortunately did not stick. (Hayes Presidential Library)

Looking southward along Main Street in Sharpsburg, Maryland. Both Union and Confederate forces used this road on the day of battle at Antietam. This photograph was taken less than a week after the fighting. (Library of Congress)

One of the few photographs taken during the Civil War showing an actual battle in progress. This is the battle of Antietam which took place on September 17, 1862, near Sharpsburg, Maryland. (Library of Congress)

An artist's sketch of McKinley on the battlefield at Antietam. Twice during the fighting he disobeyed orders and delivered food and coffee to hungry, wounded soldiers. (National Archives)

The Burnside Bridge at Antietam Creek. At Bloody Lane near a sunken road, and later near the bridge, Union forces suffered heavy casualties as they tried to cross. Confederate soldiers fired a blistering volley of bullets and cannon shells from the ridges above. (Library of Congress)

Though McKinley was never wounded or injured during the Civil War, he had at least one close call when, in August of 1864, his horse was shot from under him at the battle of Berrysville, Virginia.

There were tremendous casualties in the one day of fighting at Antietam. General George B. McClellan's forces squeaked out a costly victory over Lee's army. In this photograph rebel soldiers lie dead in front of Dunker Church. McKinley's unit, the Ohio 23rd, lost half of their men (two hundred) in killed and wounded at Antietam. (National Archives)

Alexander Gardner took this picture of Confederate dead at Antietam two days after the battle. Most of these men were from the Tenth Louisiana under General William E. Starke, who was also killed. They were attacked by the Sixth Wisconsin and General Abner Doubleday's First Corps near the post-and-rail fence. The dirt paths of the Miller farm can be seen on the left. The Hagerstown Pike is located to the immediate right of the fence. (Library of Congress)

total). Fortunately, McKinley was unscathed, but his actions at Antietam almost cost him his life.

McKinley had reassured his mother that he would never be harmed in battle. In combat he proved daring but not reckless. As the slaughter at Antietam raged on, the young commissary sergeant drove a team of mules carrying supplies along a two and one half mile front. Several times he was ordered back by officers who thought he could not make it. Delivering food and coffee to hungry, exhausted troops, McKinley lost one wagon and a pair of mules but quickly replaced them. The soldiers in blue marveled and cheered as the young officer darted through a hail of exploding shells and sharpshooters' bullets.

William McKinley risked his life in delivering food and coffee to comrades at Antietam on September 17, 1862. Several times he loaded his wagon, under Confederate gunfire, to feed the wounded and exhausted troops on the battlefield. According to a rebel soldier from Georgia, one of Stonewall Jackson's sharpshooters took aim at the young sergeant. Jackson ordered, "Stop, don't shoot. I have watched that youth for hours. He is too brave to be killed."

Hoping to receive a commission, McKinley asked Colonel Hayes' brother-in-law, an army surgeon, to pass the word that he would not object to a promotion. This bit of scheming was entirely within McKinley's nature. He was devoid of egotism and saw no harm in asking for something he believed he deserved. When he returned home on furlough in the fall of 1862 (his only leave during the war) he proudly wore the bars of a second lieutenant. He was promoted again in February 1863 to first lieutenant and again to captain of Company G in July of 1864. McKinley stood at five foot seven inches, and conscious of his lack of height and his youthful appearance, he grew a mustache and made it a point to walk upright.

McKinley again distinguished himself in 1864 when General Philip Sheridan's forces faced disaster at Winchester, Virginia, in the Shenandoah Valley. Hayes had chosen McKinley to serve as his aide and deliver an order to besieged Union forces. The young lieutenant mounted a bobtailed horse and made a daring dash through a heavy barrage of rifle and cannon fire. He delivered the message to the surrounded battalion, which was then able to withdraw and rejoin its regiment. When McKinley returned, a surprised Hayes grasped his hand and exclaimed, "I never expected to see you in life." Due in part to McKinley's efforts, the battle of Winchester was an important victory, and Sheridan's name took its place in history.

The McKinley Monument on the battlefield of Antietam. It is located near the Burnside Bridge. (Rodney White and State Senator Scott Oelslager of Ohio)

General Philip H. Sheridan. McKinley served under Sheridan and distinguished himself again at Cedar Creek, Virginia (south of Winchester) in 1864. With help from both Hayes and McKinley, Sheridan was acclaimed a national hero after the victory at Winchester. Hayes became a brigadier general and Captain McKinley was promoted to major not long after the battle. (Library of Congress)

An artist's sketch of McKinley carrying dispatches from General Hayes to General Crook during the battle of Cedar Creek. (W. E. Scull)

Commander of United States Army Philip Sheridan at the time McKinley was in Congress. (National Archives)

President Lincoln promoted William McKinley to major by brevet on March 13, 1865. Lincoln sent a personal note of congratulations and wrote, "For gallant and meritorious services at the battles of Opiquan, Cedar Creek and Fisher's Hill." (Library of Congress)

There were several attempts to award McKinley the Congressional Medal of Honor for his heroics in the Civil War, but all these efforts failed.

McKinley's heroics in the Civil War were well known, but he down played them. He explained, "My experiences did not differ from those of a million young men...there was nothing uncommon about it."

McKinley also served on the staffs of Generals George Crook and Winfield Hancock during the fighting in the Shenandoah Valley. In each military engagement he displayed courage, daring and dependability and, in four years of military service, he never missed a day due to illness or injury.

McKinley's record was recognized by President Lincoln on March 13, 1865. He received a commission as brevet major. Lincoln was assassinated almost a month later, only days after Lee's surrender at Appomattox.

McKinley remained in the army until he was mustered out in late July. Returning home as a hero, he was not as uncertain of his future as were many young veterans. Though he had made up his mind what he wanted to do, McKinley wrote his former commander, Hayes, that he was considering a career in law and politics. The future Ohio governor and United States president, however, tried to dissuade McKinley and wrote him, "With your business capacity and experience, I would have preferred Rail Roading [sic] or some commercial business. A man in any of our western towns with half your wit ought to be independent at forty in business. As a lawyer, a man sacrifices independence to ambition, which is a bad bargain at best."

McKinley kept this letter but ignored the advice. He went to New York, enrolled in the Albany Law School, and, in March of 1867, was admitted to the Ohio Bar at Warren.

The Union army heading home. Here it passes through Zanesville, Ohio, in the summer of 1865. (Ohio Historical Society)

McKinley's regiment, the Twenty-third Ohio Volunteer Infantry, was mustered out of service on July 26, 1865, in Cleveland. (Ohio Historical Society)

McKinley just after he returned home from the war. (Stark County Historical Society)

Two photos of McKinley as a student at the Albany Law School in 1865, age twenty-two. (Stark County Historical Society)

The Twenty-third Ohio Volunteer Infantry poses next to the Antietam Monument which was erected in Cleveland, Ohio. Rutherford B. Hayes, a brigadier-general in 1865, stands to the left of the monument (his head just visable above the shoulder of the man in front of him). Second to the right of the monument stands Major William McKinley (with hands on his knee). (National Archives)

Judge C. E. Glidden of Trumbull, Portage and Mahoning Counties in northeast Ohio. McKinley and the judge became friends while McKinley worked as an assistant in Glidden's law office. (Stark County Historical Society)

✧✦✧

McKinley voted for the first time in the 1864 presidential election when he was twenty-one years old. He was marching to Martinsburg, West Virginia, and stopped to cast his ballot. The election booth was an ambulance and the ballot box was an empty candle can. He proudly voted for Abraham Lincoln who was opposed by General George B. McClellan.

✧✦✧

There is a first time for everything. In January of 1867, William McKinley received a surprise while attending Albany Law School in New York. After eating dinner at a boardinghouse, the students were treated to some ice cream. McKinley tasted the dessert and told classmates near him that his custard was frozen. Everyone enjoyed a good laugh at McKinley's expense and informed him that it was not custard at all. Reflecting back on this incident years later, McKinley said, "You know, I was a simple country boy."

McKinley's sister Helen. He borrowed money from his mother and Helen to attend Albany Law School in New York. After being admitted to the Ohio bar, he moved to Canton with a letter of recommendation from Judge Glidden. McKinley's sisters, Helen and Anna, taught school and lived in Canton. (Marshall Everett)

Judge George W. Belden of Canton, Ohio. Belden was a Democrat but not a southern sympathizer. He was so impressed with McKinley that he offered him a job in his law office. (Stark County Historical Society)

District Judge Joseph Frease of Canton, Ohio. Frease introduced McKinley to many of his friends and helped him get started as a young lawyer. (Stark County Historical Society)

"Business life, whether among ourselves or with other
people, is ever a sharp struggle for success."
–William McKinley

CHAPTER III

HUSBAND AND POLITICIAN

McKinley's sisters, Anna and Helen McKinley, lived in Canton, Ohio. Anna taught in an elementary school and served as principal, in addition to teaching Sunday school classes at the First Methodist Church. Both women encouraged their brother William to move to Canton.

By 1867 there were nearly eight thousand residents in Canton. Ten churches, thirty-five factories, and fifty saloons dotted its streets. Gambling and prostitution were not uncommon. But the city was also an important industrial trade center. A half million pounds of wool came each year to the Canton market, and the city produced more reapers and mowers than anywhere else in the nation. Legal matters naturally arose, and there was ample opportunity for a young, ambitious lawyer.

Through the help of Circuit Court Judge Joseph Frease, McKinley met other important people within the community. Among these was Judge George Belden who, at the time he met McKinley, was overburdened with court cases. He strongly urged McKinley to take one. The young attorney won the case and received twenty-five dollars from Belden. The judge was so impressed with McKinley that he offered him a partnership in his law firm.

McKinley became very active in the community. Within eighteen

This print shows McKinley's law office in Canton. Notice his shingle, announcing "Wm. McKinley Attorney at Law," hanging next to the second story window. (Stark County Historical Society)

This is the scene where McKinley gave his first political speech in the fall of 1867. Taking place at Michael Bitzer's hotel in New Berlin (North Canton), Ohio, McKinley spoke in favor of adopting the fourteenth and fifteenth amendments. Bitzer, pictured here, introduced him. (North Canton Heritage Society)

months after moving to Canton, he joined the Masonic Lodge, became a member of the local Methodist church, joined the Literary Club and chaired the Republican Central Committee. While serving as president of the Y.M.C.A., he sponsored athletic events, and organized Grant Clubs in each township to help elect the general as president in 1868.

Lacking athletic ability, William McKinley did not participate in sports other than horseback riding. He supported the Stark Club, a group of young men who played baseball. As one of its biggest boosters, he watched this team defeat Wooster 110 to 26 to become county champs, only to lose later to an Akron team 50 to 9. McKinley also enjoyed watching local bicycle races, but when it came to football, he found the game a mystery. Once, as congressman, he and his political advisor, Mark Hanna, attended a Yale-Princeton game. McKinley expressed surprise and confusion and did not like it. Ironically, Canton's Pro Football Hall of Fame would later be located just across the highway from his tomb.

When Judge Belden died, McKinley took in his own brother, Abner, as a law partner. In 1869, McKinley ran for Stark County prosecutor, defeating the incumbent William Lynch. McKinley's private practice in the county courts remained relatively light during his term as prosecuting attorney. He began his new duties as prosecutor in the new Stark County court-house, which opened on Washington's birthday, February 22, 1870, at a cost of one hundred thousand dollars. Judge Joseph Frease dedicated a new courtroom.

The new prosecutor's annual salary was one thousand dollars. Court records show that illegal

After helping Canton attorney George Belden win a court case, William McKinley felt confident enough to argue a case on his own. In the spring of 1867, he defended Philip Sheets in the small town of Navarre, located about fifteen miles southwest of Canton. Sheets was a tenant farmer who worked for one John Rostetter. Growing tired of his work, Sheets decided to move. Rostetter sued to force Sheets to return. The trial was conducted in a two-story brick warehouse at the corner of Market and Canal Streets. After three days of testimony and cross examination, McKinley won the case. The building later became a general store owned by J. D. Define, and for more than sixty years, Define proudly pointed to a sign in his store which read: "In this building President William McKinley Held His First Law Case."

Meyers Lake Park in Canton where William and Ida McKinley often strolled and picnicked. (Stark County Historical Society)

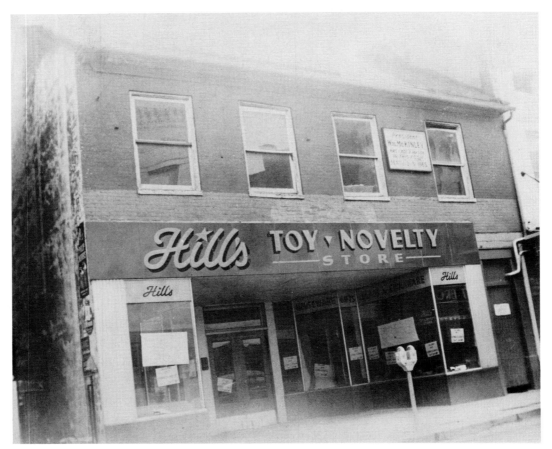

It was in this building in Winchester, Virginia, that McKinley became a Mason in early May of 1865. The building was torn down in January 1962. (National Archives)

McKinley served as president of the local Y.M.C.A. and supported many of its activities, including the baseball team. Though not athletically inclined, he attended many games down through the years. (Stark County Historical Society)

First Methodist Church of Canton where McKinley taught Sunday School and took an active part in other activities. (Canton *Repository*)

liquor sales, burglaries, and assaults made up most of the case loads. One of McKinley's witnesses in a liquor violation case was a student from Mt. Union College in nearby Alliance. He was Philander Knox, later appointed United States attorney-general by McKinley.

After a single two-year term, McKinley was narrowly defeated by the former prosecutor, William Lynch. According to area newspapers, McKinley lost because of his aggressive prosecution of liquor interests. Saloons, distilleries, and bar patrons mounted a strong campaign against him.

Despite his involvement with various church, social, and political activities, McKinley's attention turned towards another matter. He met Ida Saxton at a picnic near Canton's Meyers Lake in 1867. Ida was a refined, educated young lady who worked part-time in her father's bank. It was not until after she returned from a European tour in December 1869 that she and McKinley began courting.

Four days before his twenty-eighth birthday, on January 25, 1871, McKinley married twenty-four-year-old Ida. Nearly a thousand people, many of them standing, waited patiently at the church for Reverend Buckingham, who was late—he had forgotten about the wedding! Will Osborne was the best man and brother Abner served as one of the ushers. The wedding dinner, held at the Saxton home, consisted of chicken, lobster salad, and several

Newlyweds William and Ida Saxton McKinley. (Stark County Historical Society)

The young married couple on their western tour. (Canton *Repository*)

After taking up residence for a while in the Saxton home, the McKinleys moved into this house on North Market Street in Canton. This home was given to the McKinleys by James Saxton, Ida's father, soon after their marriage and was sold when McKinley went to Congress. The home no longer stands. (Jim Eakin)

This photograph, taken from a painting, depicts Katie, the McKinley's first daughter. She was three and one-half years old when she died on June 25, 1875. (Stark County Historical Society)

Scene of the Stark County Courthouse in 1864. (Stark County Historical Society)

other main dishes, along with sherbet, cake and non-alcoholic beverages. After the dinner party the couple honeymooned in the East.

The couple's first child, Katherine, was born on December 15, 1871. This was a joyous time for the family of three, and McKinley took on a part-time job in his father-in-law's bank to supplement his income.

While McKinley was working in the bank in 1873, tragedy struck when his second daughter, Ida, suddenly died. She was not yet five months old. This loss, combined with the deaths of Ida's mother and grandfather, took its toll on the beautiful, radiant Mrs. McKinley. Grief visited the McKinleys again when their first born daughter, Katie, died in 1875, leaving the couple childless.

McKinley settled into his law practice while working as a bank manager. When his friend Rutherford B. Hayes ran for governor in 1875, McKinley spearheaded the campaign in northeast Ohio. In 1876 he helped reorganize the Diebold Safe and Lock Company which faced bankruptcy and a proposed move back to its original site in Chicago. At the same time, coal miners near Massillon went on strike with considerable rioting, bloodshed, and destruction of property. Governor Hayes sent in the militia as public opinion ran high against the miners. Nonetheless, McKinley volunteered to defend the miners, free of charge. This won him strong labor support and, more importantly, attracted the attention of an opponent, Mark Hanna, who was an owner of the mining company. McKinley gained a favorable court decision for the miners and soon set his sights on Washington. 🔳

Canton was a growing community in the second half of the nineteenth century. (Stark County Historical Society)

Date of picture July 31, 1886. (Karl R. Harsh collection)

William McKinley was a shrewd lawyer. In one of his more celebrated cases he defended a surgeon who was being sued for malpractice. The opposing lawyer maintained that, due to improper surgical techniques, his client's leg was bowed. When McKinley's turn to speak came, he called the plaintiff up to the stand and had him roll up his pant legs, revealing that both legs were bowed. The case was dismissed and the bowlegged man walked away without receiving any financial settlement.

General Ulysses S. Grant. In 1868 McKinley organized Grant Clubs throughout Stark County to help elect the Ohio general as the eighteenth president. (Stark County Historical Society)

Rutherford B. Hayes once warned McKinley about the trappings of politics and advised him, "Men in political life must be ambitious."

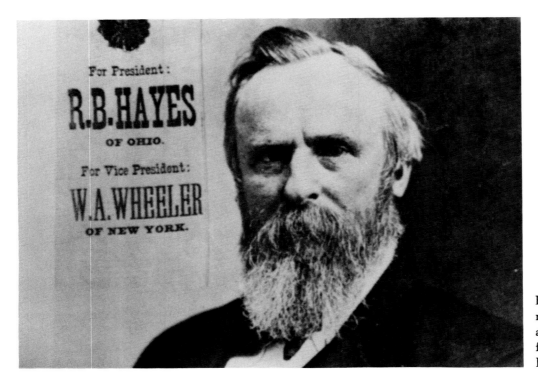

Rutherford Birchard Hayes, the nineteenth president. McKinley and Hayes were the closest of friends. (Hayes Presidential Library)

McKinley as a Canton **attorney.** (Canton *Repository)*

This sleigh was owned by William McKinley and is on display at the McKinley Museum in Niles. (National McKinley Birthplace Memorial)

A piano used by the McKinley family. (National McKinley Birthplace Memorial)

30

CHAPTER IV

CONGRESSMAN AND GOVERNOR

Following his defeat for re-election as Stark County prosecutor in 1871, McKinley resumed his private law practice. He remained politically active and spent much time with his family. Campaigning for Republican candidates, he also took an active part in promoting his friend Rutherford B. Hayes' 1876 bid for the White House. That same year McKinley was elected to the United States House of Representatives over Democrat Levi Lamborn of Alliance. McKinley's service came at considerable personal sacrifice. His income decreased by half.

His new salary was five thousand dollars a year, a financial hardship he and Ida endured. While in Washington, the McKinleys stayed away from the glittering social scene. They did visit the Hayes family frequently at the White House and, whenever Ida felt up to it, James and Lucretia Garfield, at their Washington home. President Hayes urged McKinley to initiate higher tariffs. The young congressman never forgot the lessons of his father's struggle with iron-making. Cheap, imported iron had ruined domestic production, and the McKinleys suffered. "Reduce tariffs," McKinley said, "and labor is the first to suffer." While working as an advocate of American protectionism, he took time in 1880 to campaign for Ohioan James A. Garfield and succeeded him on the

McKinley as a United States Congressman. McKinley's good looks were complemented by his sandy-colored hair and green eyes (with a tint of gray). (Stark County Historical Society)

Interior of McKinley's Saxton house third floor study. Notice the spittoon under the small table. McKinley occasionally chewed tobacco and enjoyed smoking cigars except in Ida's presence. (Canton *Repository*)

McKinley stands next to his brother Abner. (Canton *Repository*)

Sister-in-law, Mrs. Abner McKinley (Anna). (Stark County Historical Society)

James A. Garfield and William McKinley became good friends when they both served in Congress. Garfield recalled that McKinley's aim, when spitting tobacco juice into a cuspidor, "was remarkably good."

President-elect James A. Garfield in 1880. McKinley campaigned hard for his election. Garfield served as our twentieth president. He and McKinley shared much in common. Both were Ohioans who served in the Civil War, became teachers and lawyers, served in Congress and were assassinated. (Lake County Historical Society)

McKinley's cousin and closest friend Will Osborne. This photograph was taken in the mid-1870s while Osborne served as mayor of Youngstown, Ohio. (Youngstown City Hall)

This photo was taken prior to McKinley's election as Ohio governor. (Canton *Repository*)

A Congressional Memorial Service announcement for Garfield, struck down by an assassin's bullet in 1881. McKinley served as the House of Representatives Chairman of this event. His signature is in the lower right hand corner. (Ohio Historical Society)

Ways and Means Committee after Garfield was elected president.

McKinley served seven terms in the House, from 1877 to 1891, with one break of ten months. In May of 1884, a special election committee in the district unseated him, upholding the claim of Jonathan Wallace, a Massillon lawyer, that he had defeated McKinley in the election of 1882.

McKinley's speeches in Congress were factual and often humorous. In debate, he was eloquent and convincing, showing skill in gathering and presenting facts; he once gave a thirty-five page speech supporting a tariff commission. He was very demonstrative when speaking, using hand gestures while holding his notes.

Later, in 1888, McKinley was granted an indefinite leave from the House due to his wife's illness. In 1889, Thomas Reed of Maine defeated McKinley for speaker of the house by one vote. Reed, however, gave McKinley the chairmanship of two committees, including the powerful Ways and Means, thereby earning McKinley's loyalty and support.

Congressman McKinley favored sound fiscal policies supporting coined money and greenbacks redeemable in gold. Many Democrats favored more money in circulation, believing an unlimited supply of silver would create national prosperity. Bonanzas mined in Nevada and Colorado made silver plentiful, but the government continued to buy gold. In 1889 President Benjamin Harrison supported the issuing of dollars backed by silver, and Americans turned in their silver for gold, decreasing the government's gold supply. Not until the discovery of gold in Alaska in the 1890s did the nation's supply increase. By then

When William McKinley announced that he was running for United States Congress in 1876, he initially had much competition. Four other Republicans, including his old friend Judge Joseph Frease, vied for the seat. In early August Judge Frease and another candidate withdrew from the competition. When the Republican County Convention was held in Alliance, Ohio, ninety-nine delegates voted for McKinley–fourteen more than he needed. This put to rest the speculation that he could not win as a Republican because he had defended striking coal miners after they rioted and destroyed company property near Massillon. He debated his Democratic opponent, Levi Lamborn, so well that Lamborn cancelled two other scheduled debates. McKinley won by a thirty-three hundred vote majority over Lamborn in the fall election, while every other Stark County office went Democratic.

"With me this position is a deep conviction, not a theory"

Both of these sketches of Congressman McKinley come from *Frank Leslie's Illustrated* newspaper, May 24, 1890. He is shown dealing with the tariff issue. (Canton *Repository*)

During his early years in Congress, McKinley was offered a lucrative position as a lawyer for a western railroad company at an annual salary of twenty-five thousand dollars. Though this was three times the amount he earned in Congress, he turned the offer down.

As a House member, McKinley fought hard to establish tariffs to protect American industry. He became known as "The Napoleon of Protection." This cartoon was captioned "The Two Bills–A combination that is hard to beat." (Stark County Historical Society)

As a member of Congress, McKinley attracted national attention for his strong stand on establishing high protective tariffs. This October 4, 1890 cover of *Judge* is captioned: "Nobody's Pet," with McKinley inquiring, "Say! Does anybody own this cat?" (*Judge* magazine)

McKinley was president and officially placed the United States on the gold standard.

Most farmers opposed both tariffs and the gold standard. Silver-backed dollars made debts easier for farmers to pay. By 1893, while McKinley served as Ohio governor, the country faced panic and unemployment. But during his term in the White House, farmers and factory workers alike saw a slow rise in prosperity.

McKinley established a reputation as a hard working congressman, but a couple of his races for re-election were very close. Once during a debate over a tariff bill in Congress, a fellow legislator from Illinois reminded him of his narrow victory within his Democratic Ohio district. McKinley responded, "I speak for the workingmen of my district, the workingmen of Ohio, and of the country." Representative Springer suddenly rose and shouted, "They did not speak for you very largely in the last election!" Amidst a hushed house, McKinley responded, "Ah, my friend, my fidelity to my constituents is not measured by the support they give me!" Applause broke out as McKinley continued his speech.

Some critics of McKinley maintained that his tariff bill helped create a decrease in revenue, which in turn forced President Grover Cleveland to borrow money to replenish depleted gold reserves. During 1893 and 1894 there was a federal deficit of $69,000,000. Others, however, claimed that if tariffs were left undisturbed there would eventually be sufficient income for the federal government.

McKinley failed to gain re-election to congress in 1890. For the third time in his career as congressman, McKinley saw Democrats

Levi Lamborn of Alliance, Ohio, was related to Ulysses S. Grant, but his politics differed from those of the eighteenth president. As a Democrat he once ran for the Senate and had several times debated Republican candidates for office. Lamborn was a doctor, banker, real estate developer and botanist. He ordered from New Jersey some carnation flower seeds which had been imported from Lyon, France. Lamborn then grew these carnations in his greenhouse. When McKinley ran for the House of Representatives in 1876, he met his opponent, Lamborn, in a debate and noticed the blood red carnation he was wearing. Soon McKinley began ordering the flowers from Lamborn and regularly wore one in his lapel for good luck. As congressman and governor he rarely was seen without a scarlet carnation and kept a vase of them on his desk. As a gesture of friendship, and as a signal that an interview was over, McKinley would reach into the vase and present one to a visitor. It was in Buffalo that a little girl from New York asked him if she could have his carnation. President McKinley removed it and gave it to her. Moments later he was shot, dying eight days later. In 1904, the state of Ohio adopted the scarlet carnation as its official symbol in honor of William McKinley.

gerrymander his district, and he lost his seat by three hundred votes. In 1891, it appeared to some that McKinley's political career was over. Many political observers felt his ouster from Congress was due to his tariff position, but McKinley remained convinced that protection was what most Americans wanted and needed. Returning to Canton, he decided to run for governor.

One of McKinley's opponents within the state Republican ranks was former Ohio governor John Foraker (later a United States Senator). Foraker's harsh criticism of Senator John Sherman and Mark Hanna, close political allies of McKinley, divided the Ohio Republicans into warring factions. McKinley campaigned in every part of the state. At one point he gave twenty-three speeches in one day. Elected governor, McKinley witnessed economic decline in Ohio. In spite of the depression resulting from the Panic of 1893, McKinley was re-elected that same year for another two-year term by a majority of more than eighty thousand votes, compared to twenty-one thousand in his first race.

Ohio was a microcosm of the country. In the post-Civil War era, great changes took place in industry and agriculture. The population soared as immigrants and southern blacks settled in the state. A multitude of religious and political movements sprang up. Business monopolies and corruption in government gained momentum. Pollution of rivers and streams and a disregard for the environment were evidenced by exploitation of natural resources. These growing problems had to be resolved by elected officials who possessed courage, energy, and insight.

McKinley as the gubernatorial candidate, seated on the right, enjoyed visiting his army buddies during a reunion at Fernwood Camp in East Liverpool, Ohio, 1891. (Stark County Historical Society)

Though he did not particularly enjoy fishing in his adult years, McKinley joined in on the fun at Beaver Creek at Fernwood Camp. (Stark County Historical Society)

In 1891 McKinley debated his Democratic opponent for governor, incumbent James E. Campbell. This event took place in Columbus. McKinley, wearing a top hat, sits to the right of the table. (Stark County Historical Society)

A photograph of Ohio's thirty-ninth governor, William McKinley. (Stark County Historical Society)

Governor McKinley pushed through many reforms in the Ohio General Assembly. He urged a new system of taxation in the form of excise taxes on corporations. In taxing utilities, he incurred opposition from businessmen and leading Republicans, including Mark Hanna. McKinley's administration recognized and encouraged employees to join unions and publicly criticized employers who refused workers the right to organize. And it was during his second term that Ohio women gained the right to vote in school elections–a milestone in 1894.

A new state mental hospital was built in Massillon, and laws were passed to secure rights for streetcar workers. McKinley improved the state's deteriorating canals and secured legislation for the safety and comfort of railroad and streetcar employees. A state board of arbitration was established, and McKinley proposed laws to protect railroad workers, provide relief to destitute miners, abolish waste in the bureaucracy, and address the issue of child labor. He also spoke out on the evils of alcohol abuse, supporting temperance groups with many speeches and appearances. Just as importantly, he settled many disputes between labor and business. Firm in maintaining law and order, Governor McKinley fifteen times sent the militia into areas to prevent rioting and bloodshed during strikes.

The early 1890s were difficult years for McKinley personally. His brother, David, and his father died (thereafter McKinley dropped the "Jr." from his signature). In 1893, he faced financial ruin. Having been duped by a long-time business associate, McKinley found himself one hundred and thirty thousand dollars in debt to creditors. The embarrassed governor vowed to

GREEN BAY
PACKERS

Tight end D.J. Williams' given name is David Edwards Williams Jr.

Columbus Day Observed
Thanksgiving Day (Canada)

OCTOBER

14

MONDAY

SEPTEMBER 2013						
S	M	T	W	T	F	S
1	2	3	4	5	6	7
8	9	10	11	12	13	14
15	16	17	18	19	20	21
22	23	24	25	26	27	28
29	30					

OCTOBER 2013						
S	M	T	W	T	F	S
		1	2	3	4	5
6	7	8	9	10	11	12
13	14	15	16	17	18	19
20	21	22	23	24	25	26
27	28	29	30	31		

NOVEMBER 2013						
S	M	T	W	T	F	S
					1	2
3	4	5	6	7	8	9
10	11	12	13	14	15	16
17	18	19	20	21	22	23
24	25	26	27	28	29	30

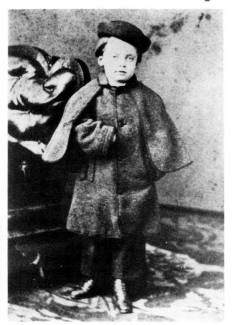

Nephew James F. McKinley, only son of McKinley's brother James. (Stark County Historical Society)

This photograph of Warren G. Harding was taken during the time he published the *Marion Star* newspaper. Harding was a strong supporter of McKinley and campaigned vigorously for him. Harding became an Ohio senator, a United States senator, and our twenty-ninth president. (Harding Memorial Association)

make good on all outstanding bills, but it would have taken a miracle to do so. Mark Hanna and Myron Herrick, a wealthy Cleveland banker and lawyer, came to McKinley's aid. A special committee headed by Hanna and a few close friends raised the needed revenue. Veterans, business leaders, laborers and supporters from all walks of life came to the rescue as contributions rolled in to pay McKinley's obligations. The governor demanded to know these contributors so he could pay them back, but their identities were withheld from him. Ida secured a few thousand dollars from her family to help pay the debts. Instead of hurting him politically, McKinley's plight seemed to have generated sympathy and trust from the citizenry.

At the time, the governor's annual salary was eight thousand dollars. In Columbus he and Ida lived at the Neil House in Columbus across the street from the statehouse. Regularly each day, McKinley looked out his office window to check on his frail wife. Waving a handkerchief, he waited for her reply in the same manner. Though Ida was not socially active like many wives, she did attend some events and even caused a stir among the ladies when she wore her hair bobbed. She cut it in the belief it would help relieve her severe headaches.

At the 1892 Republican Convention in Minneapolis, Hanna opened an unofficial McKinley-for-President headquarters. McKinley served as a delegate-at-large and was made permanent chairman. He had pledged his support for President Benjamin Harrison, and when Ohio was called to cast its votes, forty-four delegates announced their support for McKinley. He raced from his podium down onto the convention floor and protested, insisting that Harrison's nomination be made unanimous. Eventually one hundred eighty-two votes went to McKinley, who finished third behind James

---

In 1877 William McKinley went to Washington as a newly elected congressman. During his first years there he once boarded a horse-drawn trolley and took the only seat available — one in the back of the car. The trolley stopped and a woman got on board. Always the perfect gentleman, McKinley quickly got up to give her his seat. At the next stop an elderly lady boarded and went to the back of the streetcar. Another man, seated near McKinley, kept his seat while the old woman remained standing. Incident closed—until a quarter of a century later. President McKinley was interviewing hundreds of office seekers each month. One man entered the White House with high qualifications and letters of recommendation. Though McKinley had never met this man before, he studied the job seeker's face carefully as they talked. After the interview was concluded the man left the room and McKinley uncharacteristically threw the application away. It was the same man who, many years before, had refused to give up his trolley seat to the old woman. The visitor, of course, never knew his rude behavior of long ago had cost him a government position.

The Ohio Building at the Chicago World's Fair in 1893. As governor, McKinley was there to dedicate Ohio Day and attend a McKinley Clan reunion. (Stark County Historical Society)

Governor McKinley poses with dignitaries in front of a replica of the Liberty Bell at the Chicago World's Fair. (Library of Congress)

G. Blaine. Supporters shouted, "Your turn will come in 1896!"

In 1893, Governor McKinley attended the World's Fair (also known as the Columbian Exposition) in Chicago. He went there to dedicate the Ohio exhibit and attend the *Gathering of the Clan of MacKinley* on September 13. He was the main speaker at this re-union held at Jackson Park, but he was two and one half hours late. Introduced as the "next president of the United States," McKinley looked a bit annoyed. He mounted a table and waved to the crowd for silence, then remarked, "This is no political meeting. We want no politics here." He then reminded his audience that they were no longer "a Scottish clan, but an American clan." After the speech he shook hands with a thousand other McKinleys. One lady, who spelled her name McKinlay, asked him if they were related. His answer was that all of the McKinleys, no matter what the spelling, were related.

When Harrison lost the election to Grover Cleveland in 1892, both McKinley and Hanna skillfully adopted a strategy to secure the nomination four years later. During the congressional elections of 1894, McKinley traveled to sixteen states, visited three hundred communities, and gave nearly four hundred speeches on behalf of Republican candidates. A Cleveland newspaper published a cartoon in which Uncle Sam pointed to McKinley as the rising son of national prosperity.

In 1895, during his last year as governor, McKinley rented the same house in Canton (at the corner of Market and Eighth Street N.W.) where he and Ida had first lived and where their daughters had been born.

McKinley as a Mason, wearing his Knights Templar uniform. (Church of The Savior United Methodist of Canton)

During the entire term of his governorship in Ohio, and during his time as president, McKinley wrote his mother a letter nearly every day he was away from her.

The McKinleys were often guests in Mark Hanna's Cleveland home. This photograph was taken in 1896 at the Hannas'. (Stark County Historical Society)

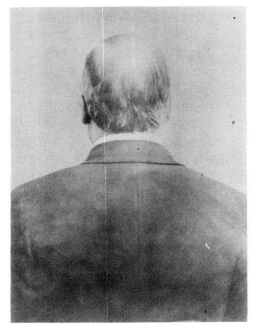

Even the back of the governor's head did not escape attention. (Stark County Historical Society)

This is the first graduating class of Miss Ella Buckingham's private school in Canton. The exercises were held at Trinity Lutheran Church where Governor McKinley presented the young ladies with their diplomas. Two of his nieces are pictured here: Grace McKinley sits in the first row at the left and Mary Barber stands on the left in the back. (Canton *Repository*)

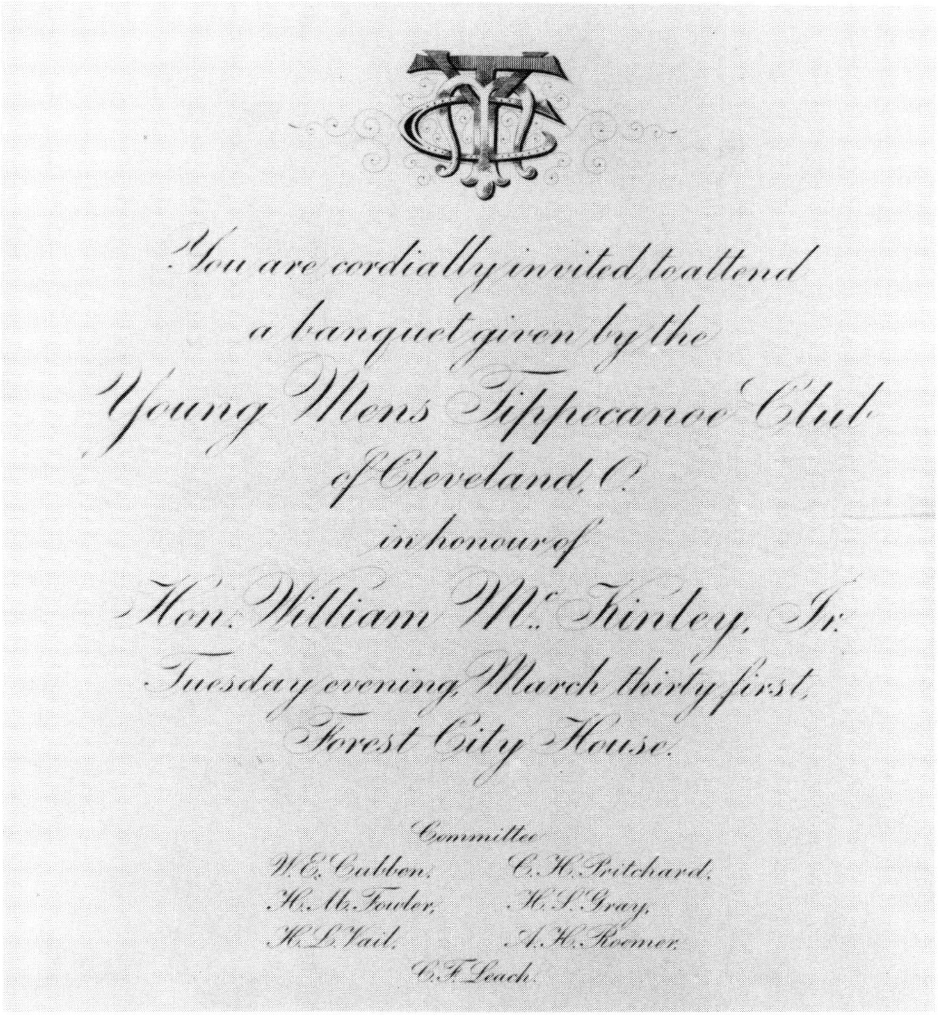

You are cordially invited to attend
a banquet given by the
Young Mens Tippecanoe Club
of Cleveland, O.
in honour of
Hon. William McKinley, Jr.
Tuesday evening, March thirty first,
Forest City House.

Committee
W. E. Cubbon, C. H. Pritchard,
H. M. Fowler, H. S. Gray,
H. L. Vail, A. H. Roemer.
C. F. Leach.

McKinley was in great demand as a speaker. This invitation dated March 31, 1891, is from the Young Mens Tippecanoe Club of Cleveland. (Henry S. Belden, III collection)

$2,000.00 809.67 Canton, O. December 23 1884
Four months after date I promise to pay to
the order of C. Aultman
Two thousand Dollars
at the First National Bank of Canton, Ohio.
Value received
No.
Due
Wm McKinley Jr

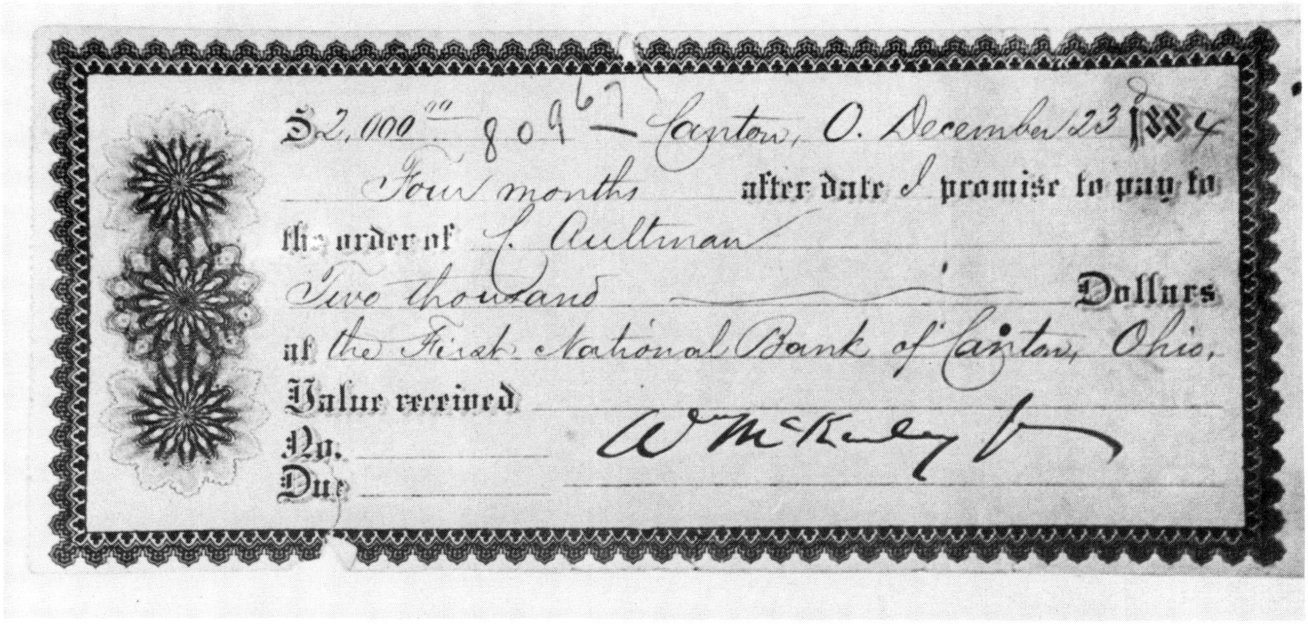

McKinley's signature, shown here on a check to Cornelius Aultman, was boldly signed. After the death of his father on November 24, 1892, McKinley dropped the "Jr." in his name. (Stark County Historical Society)

"Frailty–thy name is woman."
–William Shakespeare

CHAPTER V

IDA MCKINLEY

Ida was born in Canton on June 8, 1847, the first child of James and Katherine DeWalt Saxton. Her grandfather, John Saxton, founded the *Ohio Repository* newspaper in March of 1815. The Saxtons were also active in the First Presbyterian Church in Canton, and Ida's father became a prominent banker.

As a child Ida attended public schools in Canton and later was sent to Miss Sanford's private finishing school in Cleveland. In 1863 at age sixteen, she graduated from Miss Eastman's Brooke Hall School in Media, Pennsylvania, near Philadelphia. Her sister Mary, nicknamed Pina (pronounced PINEY), also attended there. Though ambitious in her academics, Ida showed signs of fatigue and illness, probably from overwork in her studies.

James Saxton believed his two daughters should be self-sufficient. Ida was employed in his Canton bank, where she worked for three years as a cashier. During this time she met the handsome young McKinley, still enrolled at Albany Law School. He visited his sisters Anna and Helen, while seeking job opportunities.

Ida was stunningly beautiful – slender and fair-skinned, with sky-blue eyes and long auburn hair. Her independence and curiosity were well demonstrated in June of 1869 when James Saxton sent her and Pina on a seven month grand tour

(above) Ida's father James A. Saxton. He owned the bank where Ida worked. In 1882 James Saxton married Mrs. Hettie B. Medell after the death of his first wife, Ida's mother. (Canton *Repository*)

Ida's mother Katherine Dewalt Saxton. She died in 1873. (Canton *Repository*)

John Saxton, Ida's grandfather and founder of the *Ohio Repository* (later The Canton *Repository*). He died in 1871. (Stark County Historical Society)

After visiting Shakespeare's home at Stratford-on-Avon in July of 1869, young Ida Saxton wrote her parents, "We saw the old house Shakespeare was born in, it is a very old looking place, showing it does not require a palace to produce brains."

Ida McKinley once admitted, "I was born with a peace of mind."

Mary Saxton (Barber), Ida's sister, nicknamed Pina. (Stark County Historical Society)

Ida at age eighteen. (Stark County Historical Society)

Mary Goodman (McWilliams), Ida, age nineteen (seated on the right), and Pina (standing.) (Stark County Historical Society)

Ida at age nineteen. (Stark County Historical Society)

of Europe. Their female chaperone, Miss Jeanette Alexander, was so frustrated that she almost returned home. Ida was often obstinate, contrary, and argumentative, and Miss Alexander wrote that she was also "headstrong and spoiled."

Ida and Pina's trip, at a cost of two thousand dollars each, was a real educational experience. They were met in England by two young ladies from Salem, Ohio, and John Faber, a male guide. Faber proved his worth, serving as a protector and interpreter, while he procured lodgings and managed their money. Together the party visited historic sites in Ireland and Scotland as well as England.

The Saxton sisters, their chaperone and Faber continued on to the continent where they explored France, Italy, Germany and Switzerland. They walked many miles (suffering from constant blisters), rode mules up mountain passes, took boat and train trips, studied maps, attended theaters, and did a great deal of shopping, carefully budgeting their money to buy souvenirs for friends and family members.

Either Pina or Ida wrote home every day, in spite of postage rates being a strain on their funds. Both ladies expressed a mistrust of the Italians. Complaining of beggars and thieves in every city, they took extra measures to safeguard their belongings. Ida also wrote regularly to a young man for whom she had a genuine affection – John Wright, formerly of Canton. Wright had been a major in the Confederate army, earned a law degree, and was editor of a Little Rock, Arkansas, newspaper. His sudden death on September 2, 1869, left Ida grief stricken.

In the many letters Ida sent from Europe, she made reference to

Ida as a young lady, probably during the time of her engagement to McKinley. (Stark County Historical Society)

Ida Saxton, her sister Mary, and their female chaperone toured Europe in 1869. The three young ladies discovered, among other things, that their French needed improvement. Ida became a bit frustrated when in August they were touring France and Belgium. While dining at a hotel, Ida asked a waiter for some matches, but he returned with a knife. Later, the women ordered some table oil and the male waiter returned with a cup of egg whites!

When Ida Saxton was twenty-two years old, she and her younger sister Mary were touring Venice, Italy. Sending a letter to her parents in America was costly. Postage for one letter was eighty cents — a hefty sum in 1869. Venice was full of surprises for the two sisters, and Ida could not resist telling their parents that the markets near the Bridge of Sighs were "such a horrid smelling place I hope never to get into again." She observed that all the gondolas by law had to be painted black. But above all, the worst problem was the mosquitoes. On October 14 she penned a letter, complaining she had to write with one hand and swat mosquitoes with the other. Ida, so badly bitten she looked as if she had measles, remarked, "I counted eighty-four bites on my face last evening...They say mosquitoes do not bite the Venetians as their skin is so thick, but ours is thin so they enjoy it."

Reverend Buckingham, minister at Ida's church. (Christ Presbyterian Church)

Mr. & Mrs. James A. Saxton,
will be pleased to have you present at the Marriage of their daughter
Ida
to
William McKinley Jr.
Wednesday evening Jan. 25th at 7½ o'clock
First Presbyterian Church
Reception from 8 till 9 o'clock   Canton, Ohio

Saxton-McKinley wedding invitation. (Henry Belden family collection)

WILLIAM McKINLEY, JR.
25TH PRESIDENT OF THE UNITED STATES
AND
IDA SAXTON
WERE MARRIED IN THIS CHURCH
JANUARY 25, 1871
DONATED BY MR & MRS GEORGE RANDALL BECHTEL, JR.

This wall plaque in the narthex of Canton's Christ Presbyterian Church commemorates the wedding. (Tim Wedekamm)

First Presbyterian Church, now Christ Presbyterian Church, where Ida taught Sunday School and was married. (Christ Presbyterian Church)

46

The young beautiful bride. (Canton *Repository*)

This photo of Ida was taken after the honeymoon.
(Stark County Historical Society)

McKinley only twice, in both instances telling her parents she had met an acquaintance of his. After returning home, her friendship for the dashing attorney developed into a loving relationship.

A highlight of the journey was an audience with Pope Pius IX. Garbed in appropriate black veils and dresses, the sisters were presented to His Holiness after waiting a long time. In a letter to their strict Presbyterian parents, Ida and Pina reassured them that, though they had bowed and kissed the Pope's hand, they did so "not because he is the Pope but such a nice old man." In a subsequent note, Ida urged her parents not to allow anyone else to read her letters.

James Saxton did not like attorneys, but McKinley was an exception. McKinley and Ida often met each other on Sundays while on their way to church. Ida taught Sunday School at First Presbyterian, while he attended the Methodist church one block east. After several months of courtship, McKinley proposed marriage. He remarked to Ida one Sunday, "This separation each Sunday I don't like at all - your going one way and I another. Suppose after this we always go the same way. What do you think?" Ida replied, "I think so, too."

Their wedding was one of the largest social events Canton had ever witnessed. The interior of the new stone Presbyterian church was not entirely finished and extra chairs provided seating for seven hundred fifty people while another two hundred stood. Invited guests included Governor Rutherford B. Hayes and his wife Lucy. Mary Saxton was the bridesmaid, escorted by Abner McKinley. Reverend Ebenezer Buckingham of First Presbyterian and Methodist minister D. Endsley, Abner's father-in-law,

47

officiated. McKinley's father was working in Caseville, Michigan, and sent a letter extending his regrets because he could not come. Following a dinner party with close relatives and friends at the home of Ida's parents, the couple left at ten o'clock that evening for their honeymoon. After a three-week trip to New York they returned to Canton and lived in the St. Cloud Hotel.

The couple soon settled down in a wedding present loaned to them by Ida's father — a two-story white, frame house at 723 North Market Street just a few blocks away. Eleven months after their marriage, Katie was born on Christmas Day, 1871. This beautiful blond-haired daughter brought immense joy to the McKinley household.

Matters took a turn for the worse in the early spring of 1873. Ida's mother, Katherine Dewalt Saxton, died just prior to the birth of the second McKinley daughter, also named Ida. Complications developed for both mother and daughter, and little Ida died less than five months after birth. Mrs. McKinley's condition was marked by severe depression, digestive problems, phlebitis, and fainting spells later diagnosed as epilepsy. She was hospitalized for many weeks as medical experts in New York were summoned.

Ida became a semi-invalid and it was quite likely she suffered some slight brain damage. After her release from a New York hospital she returned home, spending hours each day in a dark room pretending to rock her baby. William held her hand or read to her from the Bible during these trying times. Ida's sister Mary moved in to look after Katie.

Ida became very protective of Katie and hesitated to permit the child out of her sight except to go for a carriage ride with her husband. She often kept her indoors. Once,

This photograph was originally believed to be Ida and her daughter, Katie, in 1875. Recent sources indicate the picture was taken after 1875 and the child is probably one of Ida's nieces. (Stark County Historical Society)

Ida McKinley worshiped her husband and often had harsh words for anyone who criticized him or questioned his motives. At a White House dinner party one evening, an English woman told Ida that she loved the United States but preferred living back home in England. Mrs. McKinley scowled at her and asked, "Do you mean to say that you would prefer England to a country ruled over by my husband?"

One of Ida McKinley's "fashion statements" was wearing an aigrette in her hair. This consisted of short, cut feathers of the endangered egret bird. This style of attire brought forth protests from the Audubon Society.

Ida's sister, Mary Saxton Barber. (Stark County Historical Society)

when Uncle Abner McKinley came by, he found Katie swinging on the gate in front of the house. He invited her to go for a walk, but little Katie replied, "No, I mustn't go out of the yard or God will punish mama some more."

Katie took sick with diphtheria (some sources mention rheumatic fever and typhoid) and died on June 25, 1875 at the age of three and one-half. The death certificate listed "heart disease" as the cause of death.

Ida's health declined and her husband personally took care of her, rarely leaving her alone except to fulfill his professional duties. In addition to her other ailments, Ida suffered from migraine headaches and chronic diarrhea, running up more medical bills. Nothing seemed to help. Even a camping trip could not provide relief from her ills. She and McKinley joined friends to camp near Waynesburg, Ohio, for several days but she could not stand the noise of playful boys while she lay prostrate in her tent.

After McKinley's election to Congress, the childless couple moved to Washington. They were able to meet their financial obligations with rental fees from the office building McKinley owned in Canton. Ida went out occasionally, played cribbage and euchre, cleaned jewelry and silver for friends, and crocheted. The McKinleys became close friends with the Hayes and Garfield families, once staying at the White House for two weeks when President and Mrs. Hayes left their children in Washington to vacation in the Midwest.

First Lady Lucy Webb Hayes. The McKinleys visited the Hayes family often at the White House. Nicknamed "Lemonade Lucy" because she did not permit the serving of liquor, she and her children enjoyed Ida's company. (Hayes Presidential Library)

First Lady Lucy Webb Hayes and her children, Scott and Fanny, in the White House conservatory. The McKinleys were frequent guests at the Hayes' White House, and Fanny in particular enjoyed spending time with Ida. (Library of Congress)

W M McKinley (signature)

Grandfather John Saxton in his later years. (Stark County Historical Society)

Ida in 1888 while her husband served in Congress. (Canton *Repository*)

Ida during her husband's term as Ohio governor. She always referred to William as "My Precious," "My Sweetest," or "Dearest Love." (Stark County Historical Society)

Ida McKinley once corrected a friend who referred to her husband as a "politician." She smiled and reminded the man that "statesman" was a more proper description.

Ida in the late 1880s. (Stark County Historical Society)

Two profiles taken while her husband was governor. (Stark County Historical Society)

> ❧❦❧
> *Ida McKinley refused the use of a wheelchair,*
> *clinging instead to her husband's arm.*

In this picture, taken during the 1896 campaign, Ida appears tired. (W.E. Scull)

First Lady Lucy Hayes' most intimate friend was Ida McKinley. The McKinleys visited the White House regularly, eating dinner there and spending time with the family. The Hayes' children, particularly daughter Fanny, enjoyed Ida's company. On January 18, 1880, Ida wrote a personal note to President Hayes, "I would very much enjoy a visit from Fanny; and her picture too would be very acceptable. My good husband's time is all occupied so that I see but little of him."

When McKinley's brother James died in 1889, the McKinleys became guardians of his two children, James, Jr. and Grace. In July of 1890, his sister Anna died, adding to the family burdens.

It had been twenty years since the McKinleys lived in their own house. In 1895 they learned that their original home was available. Moving back into the house on North Market Street must have been bittersweet, but any memories of tragedy were overshadowed by the McKinleys' silver wedding anniversary. They were showered with gifts and congratulations. Ida, wearing her wedding dress, received hundreds of guests while seated next to her husband in the parlor.

McKinley was seldom far from his wife's side. He arranged their lives to suit her convenience. One of the main reasons he conducted a front porch campaign in 1896 was because Ida was not up to traveling. Though as first lady she became increasingly weak, Ida's indomitable determination to fulfill her obligations at the White House benefited her husband. She symbolized the kind of femininity that most Americans found attractive, and her faults were those of illness, not nature or character. Critics claimed, however, that she used her delicate condition to manipulate her husband.

Even as president, McKinley's top priority was taking care of his wife and he gave his complete devotion to her. This was at times a strain on him, for in addition to her physical problems, Ida's insecurity would often not allow her to make simple decisions. The first lady even summoned her husband from important meetings to ask his opinion on ribbons for a new dress or other such trivial matters. Presidential Secretary George Cortelyou related one incident when McKinley was late getting back to the White House and found Ida "sobbing like a child," fearful that something had happened to him.

With his fifty thousand dollar presidential salary, McKinley lavished his wife with expensive jewelry. She adorned herself with beautiful lace and gems, diamonds being her favorite. At White House functions Ida was usually perched in a blue velvet chair on a platform, receiving guests while sitting down. Depending on her mood, she might extend a handshake while, on other occasions, she held a bouquet suggesting she would not shake hands. Rarely did she speak to guests in a receiving line, and seating arrangements at formal dinners were adjusted so the president could be next to her, even though this was contrary to protocol.

Whenever the first lady had an epileptic seizure, indicated by her puckered lips and loud hissing, McKinley simply placed a handkerchief over her twitching face and continued a conversation as if nothing happened. If the attack was prolonged, Ida was quietly ushered upstairs. William Howard Taft told of one incident at a dinner when he heard a hissing sound as the first

Ida McKinley's inaugural gown was so heavy she stumbled and toppled over, needing help to walk.

This dress was worn by Ida at William's first presidential inaugural ball. Made of white satin, it was trimmed with pearl embroidery and rose point lace. The dress was donated by the Henry Belden family of Canton to the Smithsonian Institution. (Stark County Historical Society)

In 1892 Ida McKinley crocheted a pair of slippers and sent them to ex-President Rutherford B. Hayes in Fremont, Ohio.

Ida did not officially host many of the White House social functions, but often attended dinners. Much of her time was spent crocheting slippers (more than four thousand pairs) for veterans in hospitals and orphans. (Stark County Historical Society)

The first lady suffered from a number of maladies, in addition to regular migraine headaches. She wore her hair short and loved wearing pearls and diamonds that her husband bought for her. Some who knew Ida felt she was spoiled by flattery. She was forty-nine years old when she entered the White House. (Ohio Historical Society)

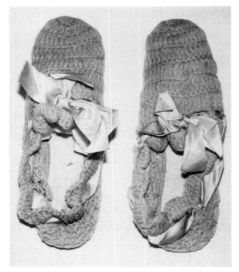

Just one pair of the thousands of slippers made by Ida McKinley. Many of these were sold at auctions to raise money for charity. (Stark County Historical Society)

lady began to quiver. The president draped a napkin over his wife's head, kept on talking, then removed it minutes later. Guests like Taft were discreet and newspapers remained silent on the subject of her "fainting spells."

Ida could be jealous, even vicious at times, to those who criticized her husband or posed an imagined threat to his position. She was likewise protective of him, remarking once to a young couple who visited her that her husband "was the only honest man who ever was president."

Seldom in good humor, she was known to snap at people. One White House visitor was amazed when Ida pointed her finger at a startled woman and exclaimed, "There's somebody who would like to be in my place and I know who it is!" And woe to that woman who dared flirt with the president, for Ida could deal out a real tongue-lashing. Though the first lady was sometimes spiteful, she was always thoughtful. When feeling ill she sent flowers to people if she could not make a personal visit. On each card she wrote a note and signed it. She did this several times a day.

The first lady spent much of her time in a small rocking chair that she had had since childhood. She kept busy by crocheting. She crocheted an estimated four thousand pairs of slippers which were distributed to friends, wounded veterans, and orphans. But when she was not crocheting, Ida often played two-handed euchre with her husband. She did not like to lose and

Former First Lady Lucretia Garfield, one of Ida's first guests in the White House. (Lake County Historical Society)

A rare photograph of Ida's younger brother George. His carefree lifestyle embarrassed Ida and he was well known in Canton as a "lady's man". George's romantic escapades led to his murder while the McKinleys were in the White House.(Stark County Historical Society)

Joseph S. Saxton in foreground. Born in 1829, he was Ida's uncle. (Stark County Historical Society)

Beautiful Annie George, a Canton seamstress, vowed to kill George Saxton if he continued to ignore her. Witnesses identified her at the murder scene but other evidence was inconclusive. She was found innocent of murder. (Emmett Boyd and The Canton Free Press)

Harriet Danner Saxton, wife of Joseph S. The couple was married on Joseph's twenty-first birthday. (Stark County Historical Society)

Another uncle, Thomas Wilson Saxton. (Stark County Historical Society)

Of the many slippers Ida McKinley crocheted, the ones still in existence are either blue, gray or red in color. The theory is, since she made the slippers for veterans and widows who lived in the North or South, blue and gray served as a reminder and tribute to those individuals whose lives were affected by the Civil War. The red pairs were made for children, many of whom were orphans.

John M. Saxton of Pueblo, Colorado. He was Ida's cousin. (Stark County Historical Society)

Ida in the White House Library. This was one of her favorite pictures. (Church of The Savior United Methodist of Canton)

usually the president let her win.

Some of the social chores assumed by the first lady fell to Mrs. Jenny Hobart, wife of the vice-president. Later, Ida's niece, Mary Barber (Pina's daughter), served as hostess at some events. Aunt Maria Saxton looked after Ida during the first few months at the White House. In spite of her health problems, Ida attended most receptions, though she often retired early. She surprised many when, on several occasions, she ventured out of town to give speeches or dedicate projects while her husband remained in Washington.

During the week her husband lay dying from a gunshot wound, Ida showed remarkable courage and composure, visiting him at regular intervals. Escorted to his bedside for the last time, Ida knelt beside her husband and grasped his hand. Begging to die with him she murmured, "I want to go," to which McKinley replied, "We are all going." Ida was too grief-stricken to attend funeral services in Canton.

After the president's death she lived quietly in the Canton home on North Market Street, cared for by her younger sister, Pina. Dressed daily in black mourning clothes, the few times the fifty-four year old widow left the house was to visit her husband's grave. Ida McKinley survived her husband by less than six years and died on May 26, 1907. ▓

For nearly six years following her husband's death, Ida McKinley's epileptic seizures stopped.

The McKinleys were honored at La Fiesta de las Flores in Los Angeles during their western trip in 1901. Ida nearly died from blood poisoning just days after this picture. (Stark County Historical Society)

A close up shows Ida looking quite ill and the president very concerned. (Stark County Historical Society)

Mary's husband Marshall C. Barber. A Civil War veteran, he was a prominent businessman in Canton. He died of a stroke at the age of seventy-two in 1918. Mary Barber, sister of Ida McKinley, died in June of 1917. She was a life-long resident of Canton, Ohio, helped organize the local Y.W.C.A. chapter, was active in the Red Cross and served as a trustee at the George D. Harter Bank. Both of these pictures were taken from an old newspaper. (Canton *Repository*)

Widow Ida McKinley. (Canton *Repository*)

Ida's remains being carried from her home. This picture appeared on the front page of the Stark County *Democrat* on May 31, 1907. President Theodore Roosevelt attended the funeral service. (Canton *Repository*)

"Destiny is not a matter of chance, it is a matter of choice.
It is not something to wish for, but to attain."
–William Jennings Bryan

CHAPTER VI

RACE FOR THE WHITE HOUSE

With the specter of bankruptcy no longer hanging over his head, William McKinley and his wife could look to a brighter future, at least financially. During his last full year as governor in 1895, McKinley had set the political machine in high gear to guarantee his nomination and election as president. Mark Hanna and his legion of political agents flooded the country with McKinley literature and paraphernalia, while the undeclared candidate from Canton remained silent.

With his term of governor over, McKinley returned home to Canton in early 1896 and continued working on the campaign. The convention was still six months away, but McKinley was in great demand as a speaker and rarely missed an opportunity to address a crowd. He and Ida "vacationed" with the Hannas in Thomasville, Georgia, where the wealthy Hanna, retired from business, rented a house for the next five years. McKinley planned strategy, met business leaders and delegates from four southern states, and took time to attend black Baptist church services. He suffered from writer's cramp after writing and signing three hundred letters a day during his fourteen-hour sessions.

McKinley's nomination was not a foregone conclusion, though his chances were better than anyone

Industrialist millionaire Mark Hanna, nicknamed "Dollar Mark." He was not only McKinley's campaign manager but his close friend as well. Hanna served from 1897 to 1904 as a United States senator from Ohio, and once observed, "McKinley is the best man I ever knew...he is a saint." (Stark County Historical Society)

President Benjamin Harrison. McKinley worked hard for Harrison's nomination and election in 1892. When McKinley ran for president in 1896, he needed Harrison's support, along with some political advice. (National Archives)

Henry Timken, Canton industrialist, who was a strong backer of McKinley. (Timken Company)

Party boss and United States Senator Thomas C. Platt of New York was a McKinley rival and had a strong dislike for the New York governor Theodore Roosevelt. (James Hyde Clark collection)

Levi P. Morton brought impressive credentials to the 1896 convention as a presidential candidate but lost the nomination to McKinley. (James Hyde Clark collection)

This unflattering cartoon by J.S. Pughe appeared in the April 29, 1896, edition of *Puck*. Representing Populist views, it was originally printed in color and captioned "When McKinley Is President." (Ohio Historical Society)

❦

In the 1896 presidential race it was suggested to McKinley that Theodore Roosevelt, then police commissioner of New York City, help in the campaign. McKinley told a friend of Roosevelt's that he was "always into rows with everybody. I am afraid he is too pugnacious." Roosevelt admitted that "McKinley thinks I am hot-headed." Nevertheless, Roosevelt campaigned extensively for McKinley.

---

else's. There was no shortage of competition. Members of the House of Representatives favored Speaker Thomas Reed, whose ego was matched by his earthy wit and sarcasm. Reed was also unhappy with Hanna's political maneuvering. The Senate, except for Henry Cabot Lodge, disliked Reed and backed one of their own – William Allison of Iowa. An even bigger threat was Levi Morton, whose credentials were impressive. Morton was a wealthy banker, a former ambassador, vice-president under Benjamin Harrison, and governor of New York. He was well respected in both houses but party bosses Tom Platt of New York and Matthew Quay of Pennsylvania had their eyes set on the White House as well. Morton needed their support if he were to be nominated. Quay had secured the Pennsylvania delegation as a favorite son while Platt, realizing he could not get the necessary votes, promised McKinley his support in exchange for the secretary of treasury post. McKinley, however, refused to make a deal.

None of these candidates nor their backers could stem the tide of McKinley support swelling in the states. Hanna and his forces worked more feverishly in the summer of 1896. Beginning with the third week of July, Hanna set up head-quarters near the convention site in St. Louis. He insisted that black delegates be allowed to have rooms at the hotel where he stayed, even though this angered southern white delegates. He then tried to garner the support of the Republican National Committee. He persuaded thirty-five of the fifty members to "stand firm" for McKinley. After a heated argument with Henry Cabot Lodge over the party's gold standard plank, Hanna announced that the delegates were ready to vote.

Posters such as this one were plastered all over the country in 1896. They were originally printed in color.
(Stark County Historical Society)

FARMER McKINLEY TAKES OFF HIS COAT.

Front cover of *Harper's* Weekly, dated July 25, 1896. The Republican candidate prepares for the campaign. (*Harper's* Weekly)

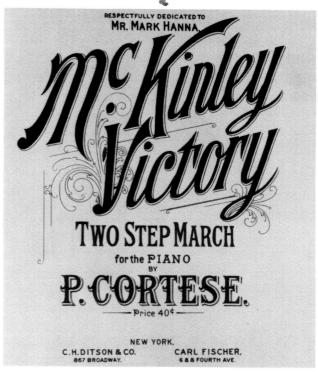

There were many songs written for the 1896 McKinley race. Here are two examples of sheet music from that campaign. (Stark County Historical Society)

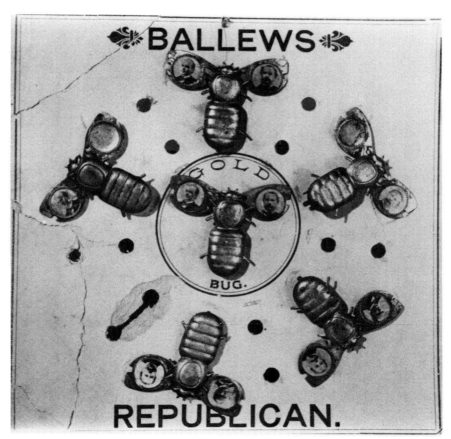

Souvenir "gold bugs" were worn by McKinley supporters in 1896. (Stark County Historical Society)

A porcelain plate showing the two Republican nominees. This item was made in England by John Maddock & Sons, Ltd. in 1896. (Private collection of Stewart Witham)

A souvenir comb/brush of 1896. (Library of Congress)

A sterling silver campaign spoon with McKinley's likeness on it could be purchased for one dollar. (Tim Wedekamm)

This twelve-inch tall McKinley mug was made in Philadelphia in 1896. Also called a "Toby mug," this one depicts the candidate as the "Napoleon of Protection." These mugs were produced in several sizes. (Private collection of Stewart Witham)

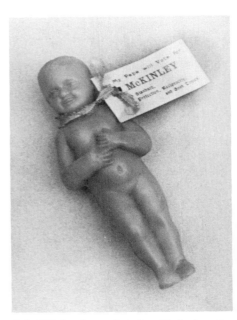

A McKinley "soap baby" sold during the 1896 campaign. The small tag announces, "My Papa will Vote for McKinley." (Private collection of Stewart Witham)

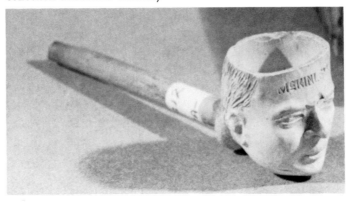

A McKinley clay pipe. (Private collection of Stewart Witham)

McKinley won on the first ballot with six hundred sixty-one and one-half votes. The Ohio delegation put him over the top. McKinley was immediately notified by telephone back home in Canton, Ohio. The news was received with a joyous clang of bells, several one hundred gun salutes, and steam whistles. Garret Hobart, a millionaire state senator from New Jersey and a loyal Hanna organizer, was selected as the vice presidential nominee.

Ironically, one of the reporters at the convention was William Jennings Bryan who occupied a back row seat in the press stand. He was covering the event for his own newspaper, The *Omaha World-Herald*, and three weeks later he was nominated by the Democrats to oppose McKinley.

The *Boston Herald* had this to say about McKinley and the convention's proceedings: "The dollar has been put above the man. Money is in the saddle. Folks have been bought and sold, some with money, some with promise of place– it all reeks of bossism and dictation....Hanna is the true nominee." Newspapers owned by William Randolph Hearst and Joseph Pulitzer echoed similar criticisms.

The campaign of 1896 was as much a contrast in personalities as in ideology. William Jennings Bryan of Nebraska was nearly twenty years younger than McKinley. He campaigned with vigor, crisscrossing the nation, addressing nearly five million people and getting very little sleep. Bryan was an eloquent and forceful speaker and regarded himself as the champion of farmers, factory workers, and Populists. Nicknamed the "Silver-Tongued Orator," he advocated the free coinage of silver. His "Cross of Gold" speech at the

This sketch appeared in the August 29, 1896 edition of *Harper's* Weekly, bearing the caption "The deadly parallel." (Library of Congress)

McKinley's Front Porch Campaign was a huge success. Trainloads of visitors came to meet the candidate. Here McKinley and his wife posed with representatives of the Women's Republican Club. Every lady carried a basket, each representing a state. (Stark County Historical Society)

Democratic convention electrified those in attendance, and he repeated it many times.

McKinley, on the other hand, appealed to business leaders and had significant support from labor. His speeches were carefully prepared and delivered in a formal style. While fourteen hundred Republican leaders spoke on behalf of McKinley throughout the country, the candidate let the people come to him.

McKinley's support in the race was growing. McKinley Clubs were formed all over the country. His friend and cousin from boyhood days, Will Osborne, served as secretary of the Republican National Committee and, as a prominent Boston attorney, distributed more than a million pieces of literature in the large cities of the East. He warned the candidate, however, that mentioning the gold versus silver issue was too confusing to the masses of voters. William R. Day of Canton, vacationing on Mackinac Island, Michigan, in late July, wrote McKinley, "I meet Democrats everyday who are going to vote for you."

Like Garfield before him, McKinley conducted a front porch campaign. On the first day of the campaign an estimated fifty thousand people came from surrounding cities and villages including Carrollton, Niles, Youngstown, Massillon, and Akron. The crowd trampled the lawn, destroyed the flowers and shrubbery, broke the iron fence, barged through the back door and knocked down a few women. Pickpockets also enjoyed a field day.

Pilgrimages to McKinley's home, however, were well planned. Hanna arranged low excursion group rates with railroad companies. As delegations of citizens arrived daily by train, a committee of greeters escorted each group from the depot to the McKinley home. Militia Captain Harry Frease accom-

McKinley's presidential campaign in 1896 kept local painters and carpenters busy in Canton. The "Front Porch Campaign" attracted thousands of people and this took a toll on the McKinley home on North Market Street. Visitors slivered souvenirs from the side of the house and damaged other pieces of property so much that repairs were constantly necessary.

Captain Harry Frease (on a dapple gray horse in the center) leads a company of mounted men, having just passed McKinley's home. The group stopped under the McKinley Arch at the intersection of North Market and Sixth Street in Canton to pose for this picture. (*Canton Repository*)

panied each group with mounted troops. The procession passed underneath a McKinley arch which spanned the width of North Market Street. An appointed spokesman made a brief address and the candidate responded with a carefully edited speech. Lemonade was then served as McKinley chatted with eager supporters, posed for pictures, and shook hands. Ida, on the other hand, sometimes stayed at a friend's house or at the Saxton farm in Minerva. One visitor who stopped in Canton was William Jennings Bryan; he was impressed by McKinley's genuine cordiality and mass appeal.

Joe Smith, a speedy messenger for Hanna, also met each delegation at the depot, then raced back to McKinley's home so that appropriate remarks could be prepared. And depending on the home territory of the visitors, the band might play "Dixie" (for southern delegations), "Marching Through Georgia" (for Union Army veterans), or "Onward Christian Soldiers" (for religious groups). Four local singers known as the McKinley Quartet also entertained crowds.

The Republican campaign was well financed. "Dollar Mark" Hanna, as he was dubbed, organized industrialists, raising more than three and one-half million dollars compared to only six hundred thousand dollars raised by the Democrats. McKinley's promise of prosperity was "A Full Dinner Pail." Factory workers found slips in their pay envelopes announcing, "If Bryan is elected, do not come back to work. The plant will be closed." Republicans pictured Bryan as a dangerous radical and demagogue unfit for high office. Even incumbent President Grover Cleveland privately hoped for Bryan's defeat and refused to endorse him.

A delegation in front of McKinley's home. Note the sign "16 Republicans to 1 Democrat"—a play on the ratio of 16 ounces of silver equal to one ounce of gold. McKinley favored the gold standard, but later adopted a bimetal backing of United States currency. (Stark County Historical Society)

The McKinley Quartet. From left to right: McKinley, Billy Reed, Mr. Lawson, Alfred Baehreus, and Thomas Malloy. Russell Chase stands on the porch behind the group.(Canton *Repository*)

William McKinley was the first candidate to use the telephone in a presidential campaign. In 1896 he phoned thirty-eight of his campaign managers, in as many states, from his home in Canton.

A visit from the Illinois delegation. (The Timken Company)

Because of her infrequent public appearances during the campaign of 1896, Ida McKinley became the target of speculation. Rumors were widely circulated in the South, particularly in Missouri, which variously described Ida as a mulatto, an English spy, a Catholic fanatic, an insane cripple, and a victim of wife-beatings. To offset these distortions, Mark Hanna and his brother issued a campaign biography of Ida — the first of its kind for a presidential candidate's wife.

Hundreds of cartoons were published during the 1896 campaign. In this one, "William Tell" McKinley prepares to shoot an apple (the presidency) while refusing to bow to the high hat of Boss Rule. (Stark County Historical Society)

Editorial cartoon showing the candidate steering the McKinley Flying Machine with Mark Hanna at the rudder. Gaining momentum, the machine flies toward the White House while party boss Matthew Quay hangs on for dear life. Thomas Reed and Levi Morton can only watch from below. McKinley is depicted as the "Napoleon of Protection." (Stark County Historical Society)

Democratic presidential candidate William Jennings Bryan. At age thirty-six he was one of the youngest candidates ever nominated. Bryan was nicknamed "The Boy Orator of the Platte." (Canton *Repository*)

Published in the *New York Journal*, this sketch by Homer Davenport shows Mark Hanna standing beside a mirror that portrays a very different image — how he looked in the flesh and his "other" side. Hanna was not the influence on McKinley that many believed. Other cartoons by Davenport, however, damaged McKinley's reputation. (Library of Congress)

This rare anti-Bryan coin was made and circulated by McKinley supporters in 1896. Cast in iron and the size of a quarter, it is inscribed "United Snakes of America" and "In Bryan We Trust" with a half-bird, half-jackass caricature. (Stark County Historical Society)

Downtown Canton during the 1896 campaign, looking east on Tuscarawas Street. (Stark County Historical Society)

Bryan (at left) campaigned very hard. Here he and his wife stop in Crestline, Ohio. (*Colliers* magazine)

Not all newspapers were complimentary to McKinley. The June 6, 1896, edition of *Harper's* Weekly criticized "Major" McKinley for his ambiguity on the problems of sound money. His initial refusal to speak on this issue led many to believe he was "straddling the fence." (National Archives)

Cartoonist Frederick Opper of Ohio had this sketch appear on the front cover of *Puck*, October 21, 1896. It was captioned, "The more he talks, the more McKinley weighs." During McKinley's first term, Opper's views changed and he attacked the administration with gusto. (Library of Congress)

The Republican Club of Buffalo, New York, getting ready to leave Canton on October 28, 1896. (The Hoover Company)

Many of the newspapers which had supported Grover Cleveland and other sound-money Democrats opposed Bryan. Some Populist leaders bolted the Democratic Party too, referring to Bryan as "The Knight of the Disinherited." Though McKinley's campaign got off to a rather slow and rocky start, it steadily gained momentum. Basically the North and Midwest supported McKinley, while the South and West, with the exception of California and Oregon, backed Bryan. On Election Day McKinley garnered a little more than seven million popular votes compared to six and one-half million for his opponent. His margin in the electoral college was a bit more impressive, capturing two hundred seventy-one of the four hundred and seventy-one electoral votes.

The mail following McKinley's election was not all congratulatory. Hundreds of letters and telegrams coming to the president-elect in Canton were requests for government positions. Many of these job seekers came highly recommended. Brother Abner, a lawyer in New York City, suggested some appointments, and former First Lady Lucretia Garfield wrote him urging the appointment of one J.J. Barclay for an ambassadorship.

Parade moving north past Canton's square on North Market Street. (Stark County Historical Society)

As a final friendly gesture, outgoing President Grover Cleveland redecorated part of the White House for newcomers William and Ida McKinley. He added touches to the Blue Room and even had his large portrait removed. Cleveland had the large square bedroom painted yellow. Ida McKinley hated yellow and upon seeing the bedroom, abruptly turned and left. When she returned to the White House as first lady she demanded it be painted pink. It was so done the next day.

After her son was elected president in 1896, Nancy Allison McKinley told newsmen, "William was naturally a good boy, but he was not a particularly good baby. He began to take notice of things when very young. He was a healthy baby."

Election Day 1896 outside the Stark County Courthouse. (Stark County Historical Society)

The polling place where McKinley cast his ballot. (Stark County Historical Society)

McKinley chats with his friend, Alexander Hurford, just after voting in Canton. (Canton *Repository*)

Nancy Allison McKinley wanted her son to be a Methodist bishop. When informed of William's election, she prayed aloud, "Oh, God, keep him humble." (Canton *Repository*)

This picture was taken the morning after the 1896 election. The president-elect is reading about his victory in the Canton *Repository*. (Stark County Historical Society)

Canton celebrates the campaign of its favorite son. (Canton *Repository*)

Two Mrs. McKinleys attend the inauguration, March 4, 1897. Ida sits on the left next to Addison Porter and the president's mother is on the right, partially covered by an umbrella. (Canton *Repository*)

William McKinley was sworn in as president on March 4, 1897. Accompanied by out-going president Grover Cleveland, McKinley appeared solemn and nervous. More than thirty thousand people filled the Capitol plaza as he repeated the oath of office administered by Chief Justice Melville Fuller. With his wife and mother seated behind him, the new president kissed the *Bible* and then gave his inaugural address. After attending a buffet in the Senate, he and Ida sat in the reviewing stand to watch a three-hour parade. That evening they attended the inaugural ball and by eleven were in bed at the White House. The next morning McKinley began his duties as the twenty-fifth chief executive.

McKinley's shoes for his inauguration were specially made by a cobbler in Canton, Ohio. This same shoemaker had been a Union drummer boy at the battle of Gettysburg.

This 1897 cartoon has President McKinley prodding Congress to move more quickly on his programs. Congress, however, is hampered and tied up by pressure groups such as Populists, monopolies, and pro-silver Democrats. (National Archives)

This cigar box, including its Cantona cigars, was made after McKinley was elected president. A souvenir metal match box rests beside it. McKinley loved cigars but Ida hated the smell of them. (Private collection of Stewart Witham)

This George Luks editorial cartoon appeared in *The Verdict*. In it, Senator Mark Hanna points to a portrait of Henry Clay who had said, "I would rather be right than president." Hanna is saying to McKinley, "That man Clay was an ass. It's better to be president than to be right!" (Library of Congress)

This cartoon, published in *Puck* in color, shows Hanna and McKinley after the election, about to carve up a Thanksgiving turkey. It was captioned, "For What We Are About To Receive, May The Lord Make Us Truly Thankful." (Ohio Historical Society)

McKinley giving his first presidential inaugural address. For the first time, motion pictures were taken of an inauguration. McKinley appeared nervous after his oath, but upon removing his typed speech from his pocket and putting on his glasses, he gazed out at the large crowd and spoke in a clear, loud, relaxed tone. (Stark County Historical Society)

McKinley and Vice-President Garret Hobart, a former New Jersey senator. (Stark County Historical Society)

At the 1900 Republican Convention in Philadelphia the delegates were waiting to see which man President McKinley would name to be his running mate. McKinley's first vice-president, Garret Hobart, had died in office. Though McKinley preferred Senator William Allison on the ticket, and campaign organizers wanted Cornelius Bliss, neither of their two choices would accept. Thus, McKinley left it up to the convention delegates to decide, and many of them wanted the "hero of San Juan Hill" and New York governor, Theodore Roosevelt. Party bosses from the east also preferred Roosevelt on the ticket so they could get him out of New York politics. When some anti-Roosevelt delegates complained to Hanna that someone else other than Roosevelt should be the vice-presidential nominee, Hanna told them, "I am not in control! McKinley won't let me use the power of the administration to defeat Roosevelt. He is blind, or afraid, or something!" Roosevelt was nominated.

Sheet music from the 1900 campaign. (Stark County Historical Society)

The Republican National Convention in session in Philadelphia, June 19, 20, 21, 1900. McKinley was renominated, and since Vice-President Hobart had died in office, some political bosses worked to get Theodore Roosevelt on the ticket. In this way he would no longer be governor of New York. Roosevelt firmly believed it was the end of his political career. McKinley had no preference for a running mate and let the convention decide. (Canton *Repository*)

By the end of his first term, McKinley had witnessed good harvests, a steady rise in prices, and discoveries of gold in Alaska. More people were working and the depression had ended. Patriotic fervor swept the nation as it defeated Spain in a brief war in 1898. Vice-President Hobart had died in 1899, and there was talk that the governor of New York, Theodore Roosevelt, might be named as a running mate in the next election.

The only question at the 1900 convention was who would be the next vice-presidential candidate. Many delegates wanted Theodore Roosevelt, the out-spoken war hero who had resigned his post as assistant secretary of the navy to fight against the Spanish. McKinley privately preferred someone else, but left it up to the convention to select a running mate. Political bosses, including Hanna, thought they could moderate Roosevelt by getting him to accept the vice-presidential nomination. As mayor of New York City and governor of the state, he had proved headstrong and unmanageable to powerful party leaders. After the convention made its choice, Hanna told McKinley, "Now it is up to you to live!"

The 1900 race was a rematch between the top two contenders. The Democrats, led again by Bryan, argued that the United States was becoming an imperialistic power. Many farmers this time favored McKinley. While Bryan stumped the country once more, McKinley remained aloof, letting Roosevelt address large crowds and advocating "Four More Years of the Full Dinner Pail." McKinley's margin of victory in popular and electoral votes was slightly better. Even Bryan's home state of Nebraska went for McKinley. ▨

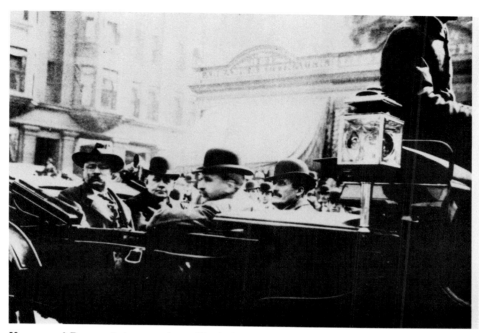

Hanna and Roosevelt in a carriage. (Stark County Historical Society)

A 1900 campaign drinking flask. (Private collection of Stewart Witham)

The 1900 campaign slogan was "Four more years of the full dinner pail." McKinley had witnessed four years of economic growth and prosperity. (Stark County Historical Society)

McKinley shot glass, about three inches tall. (Private collection of Stewart Witham)

McKinley and Roosevelt, whose picture is blurred (he was always moving). As an incumbent president, McKinley felt it was undignified to campaign, so it was up to Roosevelt to "hit the stump." He did so with tremendous energy and attracted large crowds. This photograph appeared on the front page of the Canton *Repository* on July 9, 1900.(Stark County Historical Society)

A 1900 "Full Dinner Pail" candle holder. These lanterns were carried in torchlight parades. Three candles were put inside so the perforated letters of "McKinley and Roosevelt" would glow. (Private collection of Stewart Witham)

SPRING REFLECTIONS.

Bryan was renominated by the Democrats in 1900. His urging for free coinage of silver still made him a powerful influence in the party. The E.W. Kemble cartoon above was published in *Life* magazine showing Bryan's head mounted on a cart with silver wheels. The battered Democratic donkey is obviously discouraged by the number of times it has been hitched to Bryan's wagon. Bryan, a leading Populist as well, lost three presidential elections. In 1900 he even lost his home state of Nebraska to McKinley. (Ohio Historical Society)

This 1900 anti-Bryan campaign button pictures the candidate with Emilio Aguinaldo, the Philippine rebel leader, and Richard Croaker, boss of Tammany Hall. (National Archives)

"SEE WHAT A LOT OF MONEY PAPA IS GOING TO PUT IN WILLIE'S BANK, IF WILLIE IS GOOD AND OBEDIENT."

"YES, WILLIE, YOU AND TEDDY MUST SIT STILL AND LISTEN TO NURSIE'S FAIRY STORY. NURSIE IS GREAT ON FAIRY STORIES."

"WHAT IS CAUSING THAT EXPRESSION OF SETTLED GLOOM ON TEDDY'S FACE, WILLIE?" "I'M PLAYING I'M NAPOLEON AND HE'S THE AIGLON, AND HE DON'T LIKE IT."

Frederick Opper attacked the 1900 McKinley campaign with a vengeance. He drew more than one hundred cartoons which were published in Hearst newspapers throughout the country. A book of his drawings was published during the campaign. (Stark County Historical Society)

CHAPTER VII

PRESIDENT OF THE UNITED STATES

William McKinley would be no caretaker chief executive. He would not be content like some of his predecessors to let Congress run the country. McKinley restored respect to the office, demonstrating a willingness to work with others. Though not often compromising, he observed the custom of consultation with advisors and, with reason, cordiality, and dignity, established good working relationships. He was able to win over many political opponents with his candor and integrity. His adversaries usually lost, not in one decisive stroke, but by innumerable wounds.

The new president was gracious but not informal. He avoided personal protection, shrugging off the Secret Service to walk freely through the streets of Washington like an ordinary citizen. During his administration, the public could once again stroll through the White House gardens. Reporters noted a more relaxed atmosphere, even though McKinley granted no interviews to the press. His private life was nobody's business and he took strides to safeguard his wife's privacy as well. The press acquiesced, even agreeing not to photograph him while smoking cigars (often two or three dozen a day) because he felt it set a bad example for children. Nor did he smoke or chew tobacco in Ida's presence, knowing she disapproved.

The twenty-fifth president of the United States. (Canton *Repository*)

> On March 4, 1897, President Cleveland and President-elect McKinley were the first chief executives to appear in motion pictures.

81

Inauguration Day, 1897. Chief Justice Fuller has just administered the oath of office and watched McKinley kiss the *Bible*. Grover Cleveland, in pain from gout, looked on. (Canton *Repository*)

Part of the estimated crowd of thirty thousand watch McKinley deliver his inaugural address. He was sworn in at 1:20 p.m. on March 4, 1897. (Stark County Historical Society)

The Pension Building where both McKinley inaugural balls were held. Today it is called the National Building Museum. (Stark County Historical Society)

At both inaugural ceremonies in the Pension Office Building, the president, vice-president, and their wives sat in this special box overlooking the crowd. (Library of Congress)

Luncheon setting in the Senate for the new president and vice-president, their wives, and guests. (Stark County Historical Society)

McKinley was the second president to have his mother present at his inauguration (Garfield was the first).

McKinley was the first incumbent president to ride in an automobile, a Stanley Steamer.

This drawing appeared in *Harper's* Weekly in 1896, depicting guests at the Inaugural Ball. (Library of Congress)

McKinley's first inauguration was a splendid affair, made possible by General Horace Porter who served as grand parade marshall. After his inaugural address, McKinley attended a buffet in the Senate, eating a corned-beef sandwich on a roll, a bit of salad, and drinking a cup of coffee. The president then returned outside where he sat in the reviewing stand to watch a three-hour parade. Ida stayed just a few minutes. Back at the White House the first family watched a fireworks display and at 9:40 p.m. they and the Hobarts arrived at the Old Pension Building where five thousand invited paid guests awaited. The president and vice-president sat on display in an upper balcony while those below feasted on oysters (both boiled and raw), chicken, turtle, lobster and crab salads, beef tongue, ham, turkey, sweetbreads, ice cream, punch, fruit, coffee and assorted cakes. A dance followed, but the first lady was tired and by 11:00 p.m. the McKinleys were in bed in their new residence.

McKinley desired an administration of honesty and efficiency, but some of his cabinet choices proved an embarrassment. He appointed the aging Senator John Sherman of Ohio as secretary of state. This drew criticism because some believed this move was designed to free the Senate seat for Mark Hanna. When war with Spain was declared, Sherman's senility proved a liability, but McKinley supported him and tolerated his ineptness until a change was necessary.

William R. Day of Canton was the assistant secretary of state, but in actuality served in the ailing Sherman's place. He gave up a lucrative law practice to assume the post. Diplomats and other officials dealt directly with Day, who was careful not to usurp Sherman. Thin, pale, and shy, Day replaced Sherman but later resigned to negotiate the Treaty of Paris with the Spanish in September of 1898. Day later became an associate justice of the United States Supreme Court, appointed by Theodore Roosevelt in 1904.

Other cabinet selections included Lyman Gage of Chicago as secretary of the treasury, Cornelius Bliss of New York as secretary of the interior, John Long of Massachusetts as secretary of the navy, James Gary of Maryland as postmaster general, James Wilson of Iowa as secretary of agriculture, and Russell Alger of Michigan as secretary of war. Judge Joseph McKenna of California was selected as attorney general. McKenna was a Catholic and McKinley was under pressure from Protestants and several Republican leaders to withdraw his appointment but the president remained firm and got his way.

The ending of the Spanish-American War brought other changes in the cabinet. John Hay,

William R. Day was from Ravenna, Ohio. He moved to Canton where he practiced law and befriended McKinley. He served as secretary of state prior to negotiating the Paris Peace Treaty ending the Spanish-American War. Appointed by Theodore Roosevelt as a supreme court justice, Day also served as a trustee of the McKinley Memorial Association. Following his death, an elementary school in Canton was named in his honor. (Canton *Repository*)

Myron T. Herrick, friend and advisor to McKinley. Herrick served as ambassador to France and later governor of Ohio. (Canton *Repository*)

Lyman Gage of Illinois. A Chicago bank president and a Gold Democrat, Gage bolted his party in 1896 to support McKinley. As secretary of the treasury he instituted a sound money policy and eased restrictions on national banks. (Canton *Repository*)

John M. Hay. Born in Indiana, Hay graduated from Brown University and worked as President Lincoln's private secretary. He wrote several books and once worked for a newspaper. Hay resigned as McKinley's ambassador to Great Britain to replace Day as secretary of state. One of our nation's greatest diplomats, Hay stayed on in the Roosevelt administration and helped prepare the way for building the Panama Canal. (Stark County Historical Society)

George Cortelyou of New York was First Lady Francis Cleveland's private secretary. Under McKinley he worked as an assistant to Addison Porter at the White House in 1897. When the high strung Porter resigned due to illness, Cortelyou replaced him as McKinley's personal secretary and, during the administration of Theodore Roosevelt, he served as commerce and labor secretary, postmaster general and secretary of the treasury. (Stark County Historical Society)

Attorney General John Griggs. He replaced Joseph McKenna, who was appointed to the supreme court by McKinley. (Library of Congress)

John D. Long of Massachusetts was the secretary of the navy. His assistant was Theodore Roosevelt, who resigned to fight in the war against Spain. Roosevelt kept Long in the cabinet when he became president. (Stark County Historical Society)

Elihu Root of New York proved a great secretary of war. He replaced Russell Alger in 1899 and took charge of administering the territories acquired after the Spanish-American War. Along with John Hay and President McKinley, he helped formulate the Open Door Policy. (*Colliers* magazine)

Charles Emory Smith became postmaster general in 1898 after James Gary retired.(National Archives)

Philander C. Knox of Pennsylvania was McKinley's third attorney general. He attended Mt. Union College in Alliance, Ohio, and met McKinley in the late 1860s. (Stark County Historical Society)

William Howard Taft of Cincinnati. McKinley appointed him as governor of the Philippines after the war. Taft said of McKinley, "He had such a good heart that the right thing to do always occurred to him." Taft is the only American to hold the two highest offices in the land, president and chief justice of the United States Supreme Court, appointed by Warren G. Harding. (National Archives)

former private secretary to President Lincoln, gave up his ambassadorship to Great Britain to replace Day as secretary of state. Russell Alger resigned amid reports of gross inefficiency and was succeeded by the capable Elihu Root. McKenna resigned for a seat on the United States Supreme Court and was replaced by New Jersey Governor John Griggs. When Griggs stepped down as attorney general, Philander C. Knox of Pennsylvania assumed the office. In 1898 Charles Emory Smith of Pennsylvania became postmaster general, curbing frauds in the mail delivery system. Ethan Allen Hitchcock of Missouri gave up his post as minister to Russia to join the cabinet as secretary of the interior in 1898, replacing Bliss.

Two other issues confronting the McKinley administration were civil rights violations in the South and civil service reform. Both problems became a source of frustration within the McKinley presidency.

The Pendleton Act had established guidelines and examinations for the selection of government workers in the early 1880s. It became law after Charles Guiteau, a deranged office seeker, gunned down President James A. Garfield in 1881. The Pendleton Act, however, applied to fewer than ten per cent of federal positions.

President McKinley in his private railroad car. (*Judge* magazine)

McKinley and dignitaries in Asheville, North Carolina, in 1897. (Library of Congress)

McKinley, like his predecessors, devoted long hours to the spoils system, having to deal with swarms of job seekers. As president he rewarded his people well. He issued orders to extend the merit system but then tried to exempt a number of positions from competitive testing. Democrats grumbled, and anti-Hanna Republicans publicly attacked him for what they believed was a complete disregard for the law.

Among the most vocal critics was Carl Shurz, a Civil War hero, former United States senator and cabinet member, and liberal Republican newspaper editor. He prodded McKinley to select individuals solely on their merits and qualifications. The president would not budge but still gave the impression, at least to some, that he supported reform. One Republican newspaper agreed, stating, "...McKinley has strengthened the civil service law instead of weakening it."

Atrocities in the South against blacks and other minorities were commonplace. During the decade of the 1890s, two thousand negroes were murdered and hundreds more were tortured. During McKinley's first term the lynching of scores of blacks by the Ku Klux Klan and the murder of two Roman Catholic Italians in Mississippi disturbed the president. In the latter case the Italian Embassy in the United States lodged a formal protest. Though such events did not go unnoticed, attempts to resolve the problem were superficial. T. Thomas Fortune, a leading black spokesman, described McKinley as "a man of jelly, who would turn us all loose to the mob and not say a word."

As president, McKinley devoted much time to reconciling differences not healed by the Civil War.

In October of 1898 the president and first lady visited Camp Meade, Pennsylvania. Webb Hayes (on the left), Medal of Honor recipient and son of the nineteenth president, escorted them. (Stark County Historical Society)

William McKinley was a big baseball fan, but he missed out on a golden opportunity to make baseball history. As the Canton Y.M.C.A. president, the young lawyer enthusiastically supported the local championship team, and as governor of Ohio he threw out the first ball of the season at Columbus in 1892. Under manager Gus Schmelz, the Columbus team went on to win the Western League pennant. On April 19, 1897, President William McKinley greeted the Washington Senators in the oval office. The team's manager was none other than Gus Schmelz. He suggested McKinley throw out the first ball at the opener five days later and perhaps bless the team with another championship. McKinley replied that if he were able, he would repeat the performance at National Park. A presidential box was erected, adorned with flags. More than one hundred members of Congress showed up, but McKinley did not. The Washington Star noted, "President McKinley disappointed the seven thousand spectators at the opening game by failing to appear, and the Senators disappointed them by losing to Brooklyn five to four." McKinley missed a chance to become the first president to toss out a ball on opening day in the major leagues. That honor went to William Howard Taft in 1910.

The following six photographs show the interior of the White House as it looked during McKinley's term of office. Corridor with Tiffany glass screen. (Stark County Historical Society)

As first lady, Ida McKinley purchased expensive jewelry and furniture. She bought most of her items at a Washington, D.C. shop owned and operated by Norman and Edith Galt. Edith met Mrs. McKinley several times and years later after her husband Norman died, Mrs. Galt met a widower and married him. Mrs. Galt's second husband was President Woodrow Wilson. Through her contacts with Ida McKinley and other first ladies, Edith Galt Wilson had become familiar with White House social life.

The East Room. (Stark County Historical Society)

The Blue Room. Here the McKinleys and close friends often gathered on Sunday evenings to sing hymns. (Stark County Historical Society)

The Cabinet Room. (Stark County Historical Society)

The McKinley bedroom. (Library of Congress)

The Green Room. (Stark County Historical Society)

The White House in early April of 1901 after an unexpected snow storm. (Stark County Historical Society)

In 1897 President McKinley was vacationing in Hot Springs, Virginia, and he decided to play a round of golf. Little did he realize the controversy this generated from his fellow Americans who still lived under rigid codes of the Victorian Age. A couple of his advisors suggested playing golf was "too undignified," fearing it would damage the administration's reputation. Shock reverberated through the halls of Congress, and the cabinet even debated the propriety of such an activity. The Boston Evening Record published an article noting there was nothing wrong with a president playing golf as long as he was "shielded from curious onlookers."

Segregation, for example, was legal and widely practiced in the South. Even though he deplored such practices, and privately said so, McKinley was reluctant to return to tactics resembling Reconstruction. Any pleas with southern governors or congressmen for tolerance did little good. Many states in the South used legal maneuvers to keep blacks from voting. In essence, African-Americans were not much better off than they were before 1865. McKinley maintained his political ties with the South, but because he held back in pressing civil rights, some black leaders turned towards the Democrats in seeking justice.

On foreign issues there was also some friction. Relations between the United States and Great Britain were strained at times. The Clayton-Bulwer Treaty of 1850 gave both countries an equal share in building and maintaining a canal through Central America. America by the 1890s had grown considerably and wanted a bigger share of such a venture. The provisions were renegotiated, and in 1900 the Hay-Pauncefote Treaty gave the United States the sole right to build and control the proposed canal. In return the American government guaranteed that all nations would be allowed equal use of it.

Violinist Joseph Douglas, grandson of Frederick Douglas, performed for the McKinleys at the White House. He later taught at Howard University and at a music school in New York City. (Library of Congress)

In 1898 the White House elevator was not working very well. It was an antique and operated by water pressure from a tank installed on the roof. Its ascent was often slow and noisy when it worked, but it was a luxury to overweight politicians who otherwise would have to climb the stairs to see the president. When the elevator broke down, which was often, congressmen complained to the White House staff. McKinley told the staff, "Let them complain. It's too easy for them to get up here the way it is."

91

There were troubles with Canada over the Alaskan boundary. Canadians complained about American infringement on hunting, fishing, and mineral rights. Lord Julian Pauncefote represented Canada and spent several months discussing the boundary dispute with John Hay. Negotiations bogged down because England faced a more pressing problem — the Dutch Boers in southern Africa. Full scale war erupted when Boer settlers fought Her Majesty's troops to gain control of the rich mineral resources there. The Boers appealed to the United States for help, but McKinley insisted on a policy of strict neutrality.

McKinley and Hay played key roles in establishing an international court of arbitration (forerunner of the World Court) at The Hague in the Netherlands. Among the American negotiators appointed by McKinley were Attorney General Griggs, Chief Justice Fuller and former President Benjamin Harrison. Issues of disarmament, as well as the establishment of the rules of war and the methods of settling disputes among nations, were approved.

Getting the Senate to approve his foreign policy and other legislation was at times difficult for McKinley. Through tactful diplomacy, mixed with political persuasion when necessary, McKinley got what he wanted. Critics of the McKinley presidency cite the fact that as chief executive he only vetoed fourteen bills. But it should be pointed out that McKinley prevented many other bills from becoming law during his tenure.

The McKinley home on North Market. After Ida's death it served as a hospital, before being moved and subsequently torn down. (Stark County Historical Society)

The president attends Sunday church service on July 8, 1900, at the First Methodist Church in Canton. known today as Church of the Savior United Methodist. (Karl Harsh)

In the summer of 1897 President McKinley was presented with a large prized melon from Georgia. It was more than six feet in circumference and was delivered to the White House wrapped in paper resembling an American flag and tied with white ribbons. Georgia Representative Livingston made the presentation and gave a brief speech, assuring the president there was no office seeker hiding inside it.

Scenes from the McKinley farm near Minerva, Ohio. McKinley's livestock included beef and dairy cattle, sheep, horses, and two pet dogs. The farm usually turned a profit; in one year it yielded thirty-five hundred bushels of corn, one hundred tons of hay, and seven thousand bushels of apples. (Stark County Historical Society)

McKinley's farm near Minerva, Ohio, was well stocked and strategically located. Bordered by the Cleveland and Pittsburg rail line and the old Big Sandy canal, the one hundred sixty-two acre site had six buildings besides the main house. His livestock in 1900 included two hundred sheep, thirty-five beef and milk cows, ten draft horses, and some hogs. A wide variety of crops complemented his small orchard of Baldwin apples. McKinley's potato crop attracted particular attention. His potatoes were popular favorites at Sunday dinners at fashionable hotels and used by local churches to raise funds. Some were even sold as souvenirs.

McKinley with his farm employees. His manager, Jack Adams, stands in the center foreground in the white suit and banded hat. (Stark County Historical Society)

In 1899 President McKinley dismissed the prospect of discovering oil on his farm in Minerva, Ohio, remarking to his secretary, "I have been so near wealth so many times, Cortelyou, that I don't get excited over these things nowadays."

Off for a ride in a surrey near Minerva, Ohio. (Stark County Historical Society)

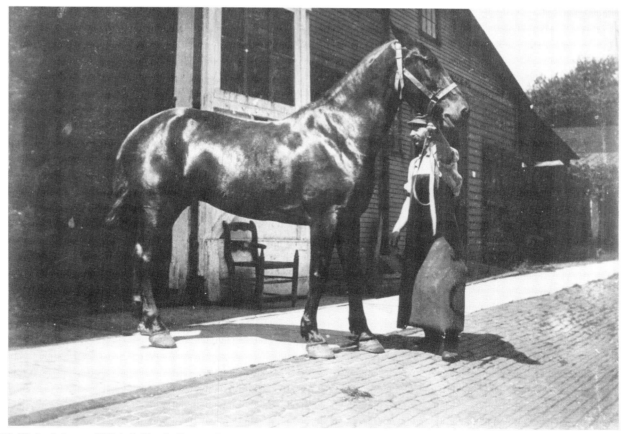

McKinley's horse "Dick." (Stark County Historical Society)

Big business helped to elect McKinley, but he disapproved of the behavior of the trusts and monopolies. During his first term as president, the federal government appeared to set a standard of reform by prosecuting several corporations and thus curbing their abuses. Though the department of justice did not initiate any prosecutions under the Sherman Anti-Trust Law during the latter part of McKinley's presidency, McKinley recognized the growing danger of numerous monopolies. On December 5, 1899, he addressed Congress on the subject announcing, "Combinations of capital organized into trusts to control the conditions of trade among our citizens, to stifle competition, limit production, and determine the price of products used and consumed by the people, are justly provoking public discussion and should claim the attention of Congress." The United States Supreme Court seemed to agree, at least in part, as reflected in some of its decisions in related cases from 1897 to 1900. Reformers were quick to point out that McKinley, however, did not pursue a more vigorous course of action.⬚

McKinley greeting a crowd in Alliance, Ohio. (Stark County Historical Society)

The president meeting part of a large turnout in Quincy, Illinois. (Stark County Historical Society)

President McKinley speaking at the Rockingham County Courthouse in Harrisonburg, Virginia, May 20, 1899. (National Archives)

President McKinley leaving Mt. Holyoke College, Massachusetts, in June of 1899. (Church of The Savior United Methodist of Canton)

McKinley entering Mt. Holyoke College on June 20, 1899. Mt. Holyoke was the first female college in America and McKinley was there to see his niece, Grace, graduate. Governor Roger Wolcott, second from left, is standing behind President McKinley. (Library of Congress)

(right) While visiting Canton, Illinois, President McKinley spoke to a big audience at the depot. In the left center portion of this photograph he stepped forward to shake hands with his old nemesis, William Jennings Bryan. (Stark County Historical Society)

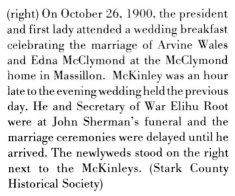

(right) On October 26, 1900, the president and first lady attended a wedding breakfast celebrating the marriage of Arvine Wales and Edna McClymond at the McClymond home in Massillon. McKinley was an hour late to the evening wedding held the previous day. He and Secretary of War Elihu Root were at John Sherman's funeral and the marriage ceremonies were delayed until he arrived. The newlyweds stood on the right next to the McKinleys. (Stark County Historical Society)

McKinley reads about his second nomination in the Canton *Repository*. (Canton *Repository*)

On July 12, 1900, McKinley posed with the notification committee following his second nomination. Senator Henry Cabot Lodge sits at McKinley's right; Senator Charles W. Fairbanks is second from the left in the first row. Hanna and Cornelius Bliss stand in the third row. Three delegates from Hawaii are also in the picture. (Canton *Repository*)

McKinley delivered a speech at the Carnahan house in Canton. (Stark County Historical Society)

Industrialist Marcus Hanna's relationship with William McKinley has been misunderstood. Most Americans were led to believe that McKinley was Hanna's puppet and simply a tool of the Ohio millionaire. But Hanna was more precisely a loyal lieutenant, and it was McKinley who planned and approved political strategy. No one was more aware of this than Ida McKinley. At a White House dinner one evening the first lady looked squarely at Hanna and reminded him that he did not make McKinley, but in fact, "McKinley made Mark Hanna." Hanna agreed.

This picture was taken of the parade reviewing stand, located on the left, on the morning of the inauguration in 1901. (Library of Congress)

Photographer Frances Benjamin Johnston took this picture of the photographer's stand at the inaugural ceremonies on March 4, 1901. (Library of Congress)

Second Inauguration, 1901. (Library of Congress)

Part of a president's job is signing documents. Almost daily McKinley tackled the large pile of papers which needed his signature. His correspondence clerk Ira Smith (from East Liverpool, Ohio) remembers McKinley often humming a Methodist hymn while working his way through the stacks of letters and commissions. Smith also recalled McKinley complained about all the paperwork, remarking, "Something else ought to be done about this. Somebody else ought to be able to sign these!"

The photograph by Frances Benjamin Johnston shows McKinley's office in the White House. (The Library of Congress)

The president poses with newsmen at a stop in Michigan. (Canton *Repository*)

Watching the crowds on the wharf at New Orleans in 1901. (Canton *Repository*)

The McKinley party passes under an archway of cotton bales at Vicksburg, Mississippi in 1901. (*Frank Leslie's Weekly*)

McKinley had just been elected president for the second time in 1900. By May of the following year, several prominent Republicans publicly came out in favor of him seeking a third term. The president, a bit irritated, issued this statement, "I will say now, once [sic] for all, expressing a long settled conviction, that I not only am not and will not be a candidate for a third term, but would not accept a nomination for it if it were tendered me."

Abner McKinley was a very likeable man. He owned two homes and maintained a lavish lifestyle as a New York attorney. Rumors circulated, however, that he was involved in a number of unethical money-making schemes. During his brother's presidency, Abner coaxed favors from White House officials. The president had enough insight not to give him any government position and never allowed him to handle any public funds. McKinley never voiced any criticism of his brother and tended to ignore his minor indiscretions.

In 1900 Ann Brewster Halsey of Elizabeth, New Jersey, contacted some friends in the nation's capital to arrange a meeting with President McKinley. She asked the president for a favor in behalf of her seventeen-year-old son — an appointment to the United States Naval Academy at Annapolis. "I have been praying," she said. McKinley thought for a moment, looked up from his desk, and replied, "Madam, your prayers have been answered." Her son received the appointment and became one of the greatest commanders of the United States naval forces in World War II. McKinley's decision proved to be a good one, for Admiral "Bull" Halsey was one of the key figures in defeating the Japanese.

Black female students marched at Booker T. Washington's Tuskeegee Institute in Alabama. Mrs. McKinley sat in a carriage in the lower left hand corner. (Stark County Historical Society)

The president addressed a black audience at Southern University in Baton Rouge, Louisiana in 1901. (Stark County Historical Society)

During his western trip in the spring of 1901, the president visited many cities. Here he spoke to a large gathering at the Alamo in San Antonio, Texas. (Stark County Historical Society)

A close up of the same event at the Alamo. (Stark County Historical Society)

With Texas Governor Joseph Sayers at the Plaza de Alamo. (Stark County Historical Society)

A beautiful tribute to McKinley in Santa Barbara, California; he rides in a carriage of roses. Ida was ill at the time and stayed in a hotel room. (Stark County Historical Society)

McKinley speaking to a multitude in Santa Barbara. (Stark County Historical Society)

Civil War veterans welcome their former comrade at the Soldier's Home in Los Angeles. (Stark County Historical Society)

On May 18, 1901, McKinley dedicated the United States battleship *Ohio* in Oakland, California. Ida was still not feeling well so her niece, Mary Barber, pressed a button to release the ship from its fastenings. (Canton *Repository*)

William McKinley refused to ride in an automobile for his second inauguration. He feared the newly-developed horseless carriage might stall in the middle of Pennsylvania Avenue, thus creating considerable embarrassment. His successor, Theodore Roosevelt, had no misgivings. In 1904 Roosevelt became the first president to ride in an automobile during inaugural ceremonies.

Two views of the *Ohio*. (Stark County Historical Society)

President McKinley's 1900 Christmas turkey. (Library of Congress)

BEFORE AND AFTER

VICE PRESIDENTIAL SHELF

PUBLICITY

TEDDY

McKINLEY

Mch. 190

There Cannot be Two Cæsars

This unflattering cartoon from a Washington newspaper shows "Caesar" McKinley making certain his outspoken and energetic vice-president never poses a threat to the reins of power. (Library of Congress)

The July 28, 1900, front cover of *Harper's* Weekly depicting McKinley's reaction to events in China during the Boxer Rebellion. (*Harper's* Weekly)

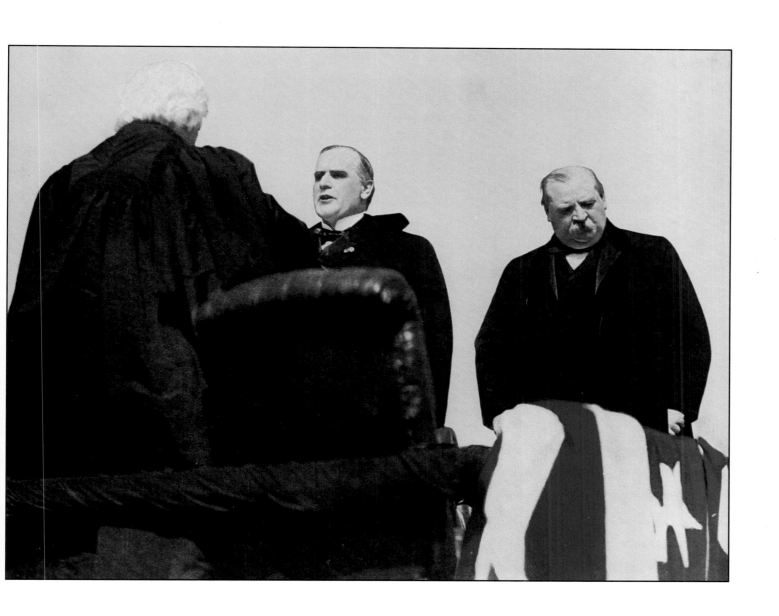

William McKinley taking the oath of office at his first inauguration on March 4, 1897. Chief Justice Melville Fuller administers the oath while President Grover Cleveland looks on. (*Frank Leslie's Weekly*)

Second inauguration of William McKinley. (Canton *Repository*)

Soldiers and sailors carrying the body of William McKinley into the courthouse in Canton, Ohio. (Stark County Historical Society)

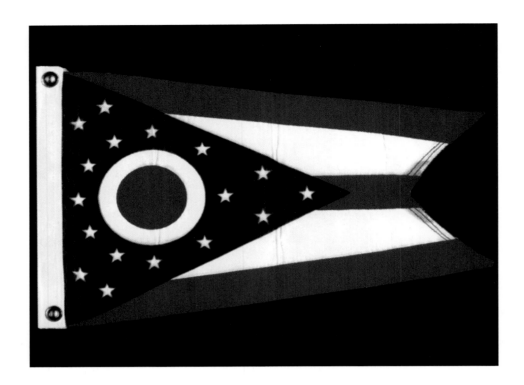

Both the scarlet carnation and the Ohio banner are state symbols
associated with William McKinley. (State Senator Scott Oleslager)

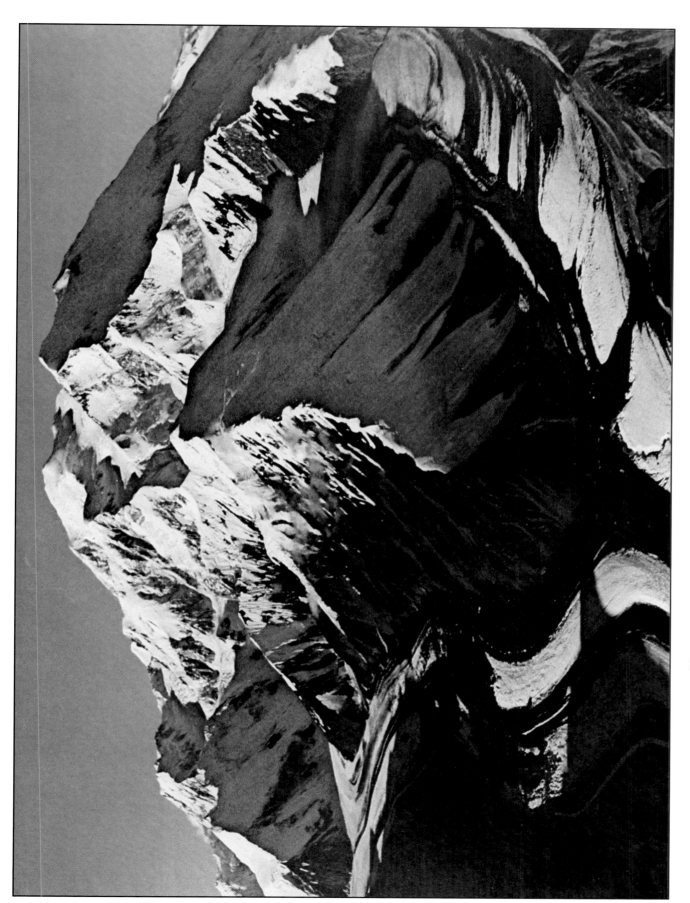

Mount McKinley in Denali National Park in Alaska. (author's collection)

William and Ida McKinley as shown on a current postcard. (Stark County Historical Society)

Animatronic figures of William and Ida McKinley as displayed in the McKinley Room of the McKinley Museum, Canton, Ohio. The figures move and talk as visitors pass through the room.
(Stark Historical Society 1996)

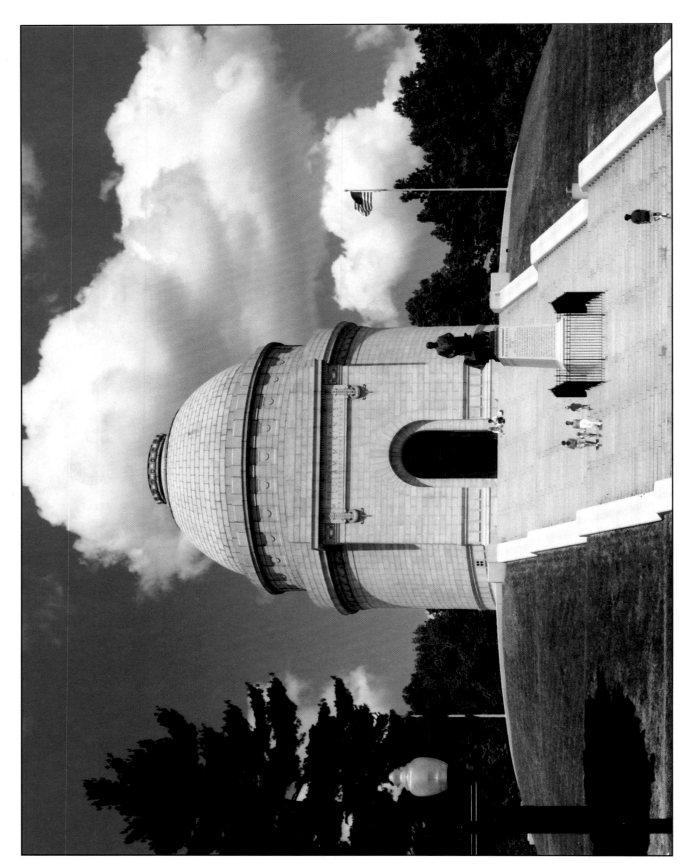

The McKinley National Memorial in Canton, Ohio. (Stark County Historical Society)

A White House photo of the president taken by Frances Johnston in 1901. Four years in the White House aged McKinley considerably. (Library of Congress)

❧❧❧

CHAPTER VIII

WAR WITH SPAIN

President Grover Cleveland explained to his successor that war with Spain was inevitable, telling McKinley, "You cannot avoid it." The causes of the war were complex and deeply rooted. Old rivals such as England, France, Germany and Italy competed with Spain in building colonial empires. In 1823, the Monroe Doctrine attempted to limit European intervention in the western hemisphere. Spain, in an effort to maintain her holdings in the Americas, built a formidable navy and imposed harsh rule on colonial subjects intent on independence.

President McKinley noted, "From the time of the Mexican War up to 1898 we had lived by ourselves in a spirit of isolation." But this was only partly true. Following the Civil War, the restless nation embarked on a policy of establishing economic and cultural ties with distant shores. "Manifest Destiny" was no longer restricted to the confines of the continent.

Several post-Civil War incidents in the Caribbean infuriated Americans. The Spanish stopped United States merchant ships (some of them supplying weapons to Cuban rebels), searched the cargoes, and seized sailors and passengers. The United States could do little, for the navy was in pitiful condition in the early 1890s. The administrations of Harrison and Cleveland, however,

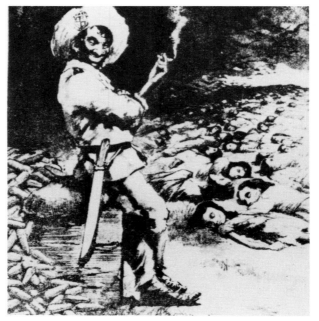

Uprisings in Cuba and the Philippines were crushed by their Spanish masters. Inflammatory cartoons depicting Spain's retaliation kept American readers at a fever pitch. By 1898 Havana had been torn by riots, and Cubans, as well as Filipinos, appealed to the United States for help. (Author's collection)

In this editorial cartoon an orphaned Cuba seeks help at McKinley's doorstep. On Inauguration Day in 1897 Grover Cleveland warned McKinley that events in Cuba would bring war between America and Spain. (Documentary Aids)

W McKinley

built an impressive array of warships, modernized the navy, and renewed the ideas of expansion and colonialism. (Under McKinley, the country acquired various territories, particularly after 1898.) Hawaii was annexed against strong Japanese protest. The Philippines, Cuba and other islands came under United States control. McKinley also settled a disputed Alaskan boundary with Canada.

The relationship between Spain and the United States worsened after McKinley took office in 1897. Spanish atrocities in Cuba and the Philippines, some of which were exaggerated in American newspapers, outraged expansionists and fueled the fire of the merchant class. The Cuban insurrection also threatened American sugar interests. Never on good terms with Spain, the United States not only encouraged rebellion, but allowed American ships to supply insurgents with guns and mercenaries.

Protecting American interests overseas carried with it responsibility. McKinley, his cabinet, and many congressmen desired peace. In his first inaugural address the president had stated, "We want no wars of conquest; we must avoid the temptation of territorial aggression." But public pressure mounted, and as Mark Twain observed, "The American people have grown war happy."

Two events stirred the anger of many national leaders. In early February of 1898, McKinley was agitated when Dupuy de Lôme, the Spanish Minister to the United States, wrote critical remarks which were published in newspapers. The ambassador described McKinley as a **"weak man and a bidder for the admiration of the crowd...besides being a common politician." Public indignation condemned Spain for**

The United States second class battleship *Maine* entering Havana harbor. Built at a cost of three million dollars, the ship was sent to Cuba to protect American interests and serve as a warning to Spain. (Documentary Photo Aids)

Destruction of the *Maine* on the evening of February 15, 1898. The explosion occurred three weeks after the ship arrived in Havana harbor. Among the casualties were two hundred sixty-six American sailors killed. Newspapers in the United States were quick to blame the Spanish, but an investigation after the war showed that the explosion may have come from inside the ship. (Author's collection)

insulting the president. A spirit of nationalism reached its peak when rallies and parades were held throughout the country. Even though de Lôme resigned, a more startling incident took place a week later on February 15, 1898, when the battleship USS *Maine* exploded in Havana harbor, killing two hundred sixty-six American sailors and injuring sixty more. Overlooked was the fact that Spanish officers helped remove wounded and drowning Americans from the wreckage.

The "Yellow Press" claimed to have inside information that Spanish agents, or perhaps an underwater mine, caused the disaster. Newspaper publishers such as the reactionary William Randolph Hearst and Joseph

These three photographs show the devastation of the *Maine*. (Library of Congress)

As war with Spain appeared imminent in March and April of 1898, the White House received seventy-three death threats on McKinley's life.

Some of the dead from the *Maine* were buried in Cuba. (Stark County Historical Society)

Soldiers and sailors carrying the dead crewmen of the *Maine* at Key West, Florida. (Stark County Historical Society)

"Yellow journalists" working for the Hearst and the Pulitzer newspapers reminded Americans of Spain's treachery. This Hamilton cartoon was captioned "The Spanish Brute adds mutilation to murder." (*Judge* magazine)

Burial services at Key West. (Stark County Historical Society)

When McKinley signed the declaration of war against Spain in April of 1898 he used two pens. With one he wrote "William," then took a second pen and signed "McKinley." He presented both pens to Webb Hayes, soldier and son of his good friend Rutherford B. Hayes, our nineteenth president.

Pulitzer were eager for war. Hearst's *Journal* headlined, "Whole Country Thrills with the War Fever yet the president Says 'It Was An Accident.' " Subsequent inquiries later showed the explosion may have come from inside the battleship, as several knowledgeable people had thought. But McKinley's and other voices of reason were drowned out by warmongers. On March 8 a House bill appropriated fifty million dollars for defense. McKinley then signed an ultimatum urging Spain to cease hostilities in Cuba and to grant it independence. On April 22 he proclaimed a blockade of Cuban ports and the next day issued a call for seventeen thousand volunteers.

These measures infuriated Spain and failed to satisfy Congress. On Monday evening, April 25, McKinley, in his nightshirt, signed the congressional declaration for war. Later a second call for seventy-five thousand more men was issued. The government raised two hundred million dollars in revenue by issuing bonds at three per cent interest. Another one hundred million dollars was raised through internal taxes. The nation was off to war.

United States military and naval forces faced many problems. Coastal defenses were weak; there was a shortage of gunpowder; and severe drawbacks in logistics existed. The navy department had no general staff and its bureaus lacked coordination. Difficulties arose in the army as well. Distrust among high ranking officers, several of them senile, led to quarreling. The

The battle cry of the Spanish-American War. (*New York Herald*)

President McKinley and his cabinet in 1898. Left to right: McKinley, Secretary of the Treasury Lyman Gage, Attorney General John Griggs, Secretary of the Navy John Long, Secretary of Agriculture James Wilson, Secretary of the Interior Cornelius Bliss, Postmaster General Charles Smith, Secretary of War Russell Alger, and in the foreground, Secretary of State William R. Day of Canton. (Canton *Repository*)

Civilians study United States Army recruiting posters in New York City. (National Archives)

Even Civil War veterans got caught up in war fever. Here, one of them tries to join up. (National Archives)

Soldiers in San Francisco say good-bye to their sweethearts. (Stark County Historical Society)

112

McKinley studies a map in the war office of the White House. (Stark County Historical Society)

During the Spanish-American War, McKinley lost weight and needed prescriptive medication to sleep. The weary president poses for a picture in the White House. He once remarked, "I have had enough of it, heaven knows! I have had all the honors there [is] in this place, and have responsibilities enough to kill any man." (Canton *Repository*)

McKinley meets with Major-Generals Wheeler, Lawton, Shafter and Kieter. (Stark County Historical Society)

In February of 1898, President and Mrs. McKinley hosted a piano recital for twenty guests in the Blue Room of the White House. McKinley was deeply distressed, however, and needed to talk with someone. Noticing his friend and newspaperman Herman Kohlsaat in attendance, the president motioned for him to come to the Red Room. Kohlsaat listened sympathetically as McKinley unloaded his burdens. His wife was in poor health; he had had almost no sleep the past two weeks; Congress and the public were demanding war with Spain; the Spanish fleet was in Cuban waters, and McKinley remarked the United States did not have "enough ammunition on the Atlantic seacoast to fire a salute." After revealing his troubles McKinley buried his face in his hands and began to sob. Calming himself, he asked Kohlsaat, "Are my eyes very red? Do they look as if I have been crying?" Kohlsaat told him 'Yes', knowing that McKinley must return to his guests. He suggested a plan: "When you open the door to enter the room, blow your nose very hard and loud. It will force tears into your eyes and they will think that is what made your eyes red." The president took the advice and, upon returning to the Blue Room, gave a nasal blast heard by all.

The president confers with General Wheeler and his staff at Camp Wikoff near Montauk Point, New York, 1899. (Stark County Historical Society)

McKinley and General Joseph Wheeler. Vice President Hobart stands in the background behind Wheeler. McKinley was visiting the sick and wounded and, according to Wheeler, nearly collapsed from the heat. (Stark County Historical Society)

James McKinley was among the Canton volunteers who fought in the war. He was the president's nephew, the son of James McKinley who lived in California and later, Pennsylvania. The young soldier served in the Philippines. McKinley loved him "as dearly as his own child." James remained in the army and retired as a major-general in 1935. He died in 1941. (Stark County Historical Society)

Soldiers await orders and prepare for a review day parade at Camp Alger, Virginia. (Stark County Historical Society)

Gatling gun practice near Tampa, Florida. (Library of Congress)

The Eighth Ohio, known as "McKinley's Own," prepares to leave Camp Alger for Cuba. James McKinley and a cousin, James Barber, were part of this regiment. (Stark County Historical Society)

Moving war supplies was a logistical nightmare for the administration. This photograph was taken at Chicamauga Park, Georgia. (Stark County Historical Society)

regular army and the national guard were at odds, and both the army and navy had unreliable intelligence systems. Both military branches needed a joint operation but were steeped in bureaucratic red tape. Supplies and equipment, including blankets and cooking utensils, dated back to the Civil War. Such deficiencies were remedied in an amazingly short period of time.

In just five months the United States defeated the Spanish and established itself as a world power. Commodore George Dewey's destruction of the Spanish fleet at Manila, William Sampson's ruin of the enemy navy in Cuba, and William Shafter's land victories near Santiago, along with daring attacks by Leonard Wood and Theodore Roosevelt, forced Spain to accept terms of surrender. General John Brooke was appointed military governor of Cuba, later replaced by the capable General Leonard Wood who had previously commanded the Rough Riders. Cuba became a protectorate, while Guam, Puerto Rico, and the Philippines were ceded to the United States. Losses for the nation in defeating Spain were relatively small. Approximately fifty-five hundred officers and men died–three hundred fifty killed in fighting and the rest from disease and food poisoning.

William R. Day resigned as secretary of state to negotiate the treaty in Paris. The treaty negotiations took time. Spanish questions at the Paris Conference were complex. Typical was the situation on November 9, 1898, when Day informed McKinley, "Our answer covered fifty typewritten pages, Spanish commissioners ask til Saturday to study it and reserve right to ask, if necessary, for more time." The president granted the Spanish more time, and on December 10, 1898, the Treaty of Paris was signed. Eventually the United States paid Spain twenty million dollars for the Philippines even though Day opposed privately annexing the islands.

"Old Glory" flies over the *Oregon*. The ship proved valuable in Admiral Sampson's defeat of Cervera's Spanish fleet at Santiago. It was three hundred forty-eight feet long, had eighteen inch armor and was built at a cost of $3.2 million. After the war the *Oregon* patrolled waters near the Isthmus of Panama. (Stark County Historical Society)

Admirals George Dewey (left) and William Sampson. (Canton *Repository*)

McKinley had decided that the Philippines could not be turned back to Spain, nor could they be allowed to fall to Germany or Japan. The American negotiators finished their work in Paris but the treaty needed Senate approval. Sixty votes, a two-thirds majority, were required for final adoption but there was plenty of opposition. Senator Henry Cabot Lodge said about the newly acquired islands, "We are going to have trouble." The McKinley forces fought hard to garner the necessary votes. Even William Jennings Bryan, having served stateside as commander of the Nebraska volunteers in the war, lobbied vigorously for the treaty's passage. The measure was approved with sixty-one votes.

McKinley felt the Filipinos were incapable of and unfit for self-government. Emilio Aguinaldo, instrumental in helping defeat the Spanish in 1898, set up a revolutionary government and united native forces to challenge United States occupation troops. Civil unrest in the Philippines soon turned into a full scale insurrection. The United States reacted strongly. On August 17, 1898, McKinley ordered General Wesley Merritt and Commodore George Dewey, "The insurgents and all others must recognize the military occupation and authority of the United States...Use whatever means in your judgment are necessary to this end." Clearly, McKinley had underestimated Aguinaldo's support, and American troops were forced to fight a guerilla war.

The Philippine Insurrection was a disaster for American foreign policy. The United States had denounced the Spanish for building concentration camps, but did the same thing. Villages were burned, fields and crops destroyed, and

Admiral Winfield Scott Schley. (Stark County Historical Society)

In 1899 President McKinley invited an army officer to the White House to discuss affairs in Cuba, which had gained its independence as a result of United States forces defeating the Spanish there. Amazed at McKinley's knowledge of international events, and aware of the president's busy work schedule, the officer commented, "You do a great deal of work over here." McKinley, with a touch of sarcasm, replied, "Oh no! We don't work any over here. We just sit around."

Admiral Dewey with his pet dog Bob aboard his flagship *Olympia* in Manila Bay. (*Frank Leslie's Weekly*)

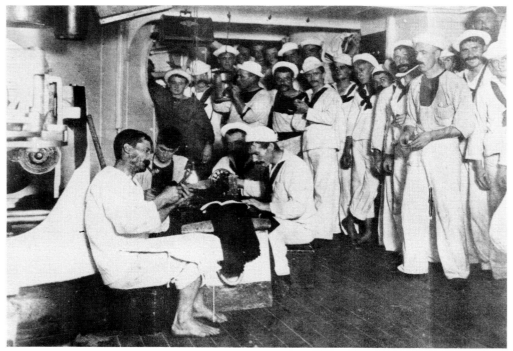

American crewmen gather to watch uniforms being stitched on board the *Olympia* off the coast of Manila. (*Frank Leslie's Weekly*)

Filipinos were tortured by army personnel to obtain information. The revolt cost the lives of ten thousand Americans, the majority of deaths due once again to disease. A staggering two hundred fifty thousand Filipino lives were also lost. President McKinley justified the costly program, concluding, "There was nothing left for us to do but to take them all and educate the Filipinos and uplift and civilize and Christianize them..." Filipino leader Aguinaldo was finally captured and, in a brilliant move, McKinley appointed William Howard Taft as the civil governor. Peace came to the Philippines within a year, but the "pacification" of these islands became a major campaign issue in the 1900 presidential election.

The Philippine Insurrection may also have cost McKinley his life. The same Hearst newspapers which prodded him into war assailed him for his Philippine policy, continuing their vicious attacks even after the rebellion was crushed. One anti-McKinley editorial concluded, "If bad institutions and bad men can be got rid of only by killing them, then the killing must be done." These words by Hearst and other journalists such as Ambrose Bierce, a Civil War veteran from Ohio, were recalled six months later when the president was murdered. McKinley's assassin, Leon Czolgosz, admitted that one of the reasons he killed the president was to stop American action in the Philippines.

THE FIRST ROUND—AT MANILA.

Uncle Sam applies the knockout punch to the Spanish Navy.(*New York Herald*)

Generals Wheeler, Shafter and Miles in conference during the siege of Santiago in 1898. (Documentary Photo Aids)

Ohio artist Howard Chandler Christy penned this sketch of the charge up San Juan Hill. (National Archives)

Black soldiers on the offensive. (Library of Congress)

Blockhouse fourteen atop San Juan Hill gave the Americans much trouble. (National Archives)

Lieutenant Colonel Theodore Roosevelt with the First Volunteer Calvary Regiment, known as the Rough Riders. Roosevelt, impatient with McKinley's attempts to avoid war, resigned as assistant secretary of the Navy and recruited college athletes, cowboys, and a variety of fighting men. He led his men in a charge up Kettle Hill, which flanked the Spanish blockhouse on San Juan Hill. He and his unit became nationally famous. (Library of Congress)

American soldiers in the hills surrounding San Juan, Cuba. The tropical heat and disease took a much heavier toll than Spanish bullets. (Stark County Historical Society)

American troops in the trenches before Santiago during truce talks in 1898. (Documentary Photo Aids)

Under fire from Spanish guns. (Author's collection.)

The *Cristobal Colon* lays beached on her side in Cuban waters. This Spanish vessel was Admiral Pascual Cervera's flagship. (*Frank Leslie's Weekly*)

The Spanish ship *Oquendo* was destroyed in thirteen minutes by Admiral Schley on July 3, 1898. (*Frank Leslie's Weekly*)

WMcKinley

(far left) American nurses, organized by Clara Barton, on their way to Cuba. (National Archives)

(left) At age seventy-seven, Clara Barton, "the Angel of the Battlefield," spearheaded relief efforts to aid wounded soldiers. After service in the Civil War and the Franco-Prussian War, she founded the American Red Cross in 1881. (Library of Congress)

Spanish soldiers taken as prisoners in Cuba. (Library of Congress)

Spanish prisoners in Manila eating dinner. They were well fed and received good treatment from the Americans. (National Archives)

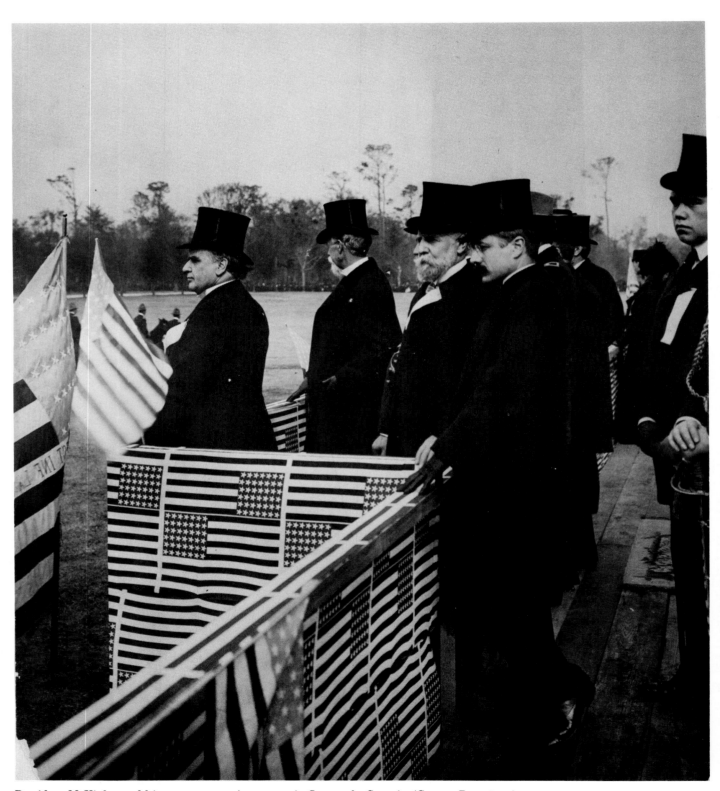

President McKinley and his entourage review troops in Savannah, Georgia. (Canton *Repository*)

W. McKinley

The president, with an escort of mounted police, approach the grand arch at the **Atlanta** Peace Jubilee, December 15, 1898. (Canton *Repository*)

Filipino leader Emilio Aguinaldo. (Library of Congress)

The Philippines Insurrection took a heavy toll on Filipinos and American soldiers. These guerrilla fighters were killed by United States troops near Manila. McKinley's popularity suffered as casualty lists grew each month. (National Archives)

American personnel at the Paco Cemetery bone pit where the remains of paupers were placed. This picture was taken during the Philippine Insurrection while United States occupation forces fought against rebelling Filipinos. (National Archives)

A native chief (seated) of the Luzon interior, posing with his secretary. (National Archives)

Filipino natives of the interior. Notice their weapons. (National Archives)

There were atrocities committed by both sides. This torture device, the garrot, was used by American personnel to kill thirty-one men in 1898. (National Archives)

One other international problem concerned events in China. In 1899 Secretary of State John Hay negotiated the Open Door Policy. Chinese ports had been occupied by numerous foreign powers in the late 1800s. European nations, along with Japan, hoped to control China by establishing colonies there to obtain her wealth of natural resources. Many of these same countries had missionaries there as well. McKinley, through Hay, appealed to the foreign nations to allow China to keep her independence and maintain equal trade rights. Reluctantly, the competing powers accepted Hay's proposal but many Chinese felt this was an invasion. A powder keg was about to explode.

The Boxer Rebellion broke out in 1900 when the Manchu rulers of China, led by the Dowager Empress, secretly encouraged young fanatics to drive out all foreigners. Chinese Reactionaries, calling themselves the Boxers of the Harmonious Fists, burned houses, schools, churches, and embassies. These so-called Boxers murdered more than two hundred foreigners and hundreds of Chinese Christians. When they and the forces of the Chinese government besieged foreigners in Peking (Beijing) and other cities, civilians (including Herbert and Lou Hoover), foreign guards, and Chinese Christians courageously resisted for fifty-five days. McKinley ordered United States Marines to China. They, along with armies from seven other nations, rescued the defenders. This international force arrived in mid-August and forced the Manchus to execute rebel leaders and destroy their forts and supplies.

Following the rebellion, the United States protested the barbarous acts of the Russians and Germans against Chinese women, but such atrocities were soon forgotten. Several of the European countries demanded territory from China as a settlement, but Hay convinced them to accept cash reparations. A few years later, Britain, Japan and the United States returned this money to help rebuild a fragmented, poverty-stricken China. These events marked the end of America's long period of isolation. The nation now stood on the threshold of the world's stage as a leading participant.

This William H. Walker cartoon attacked McKinley's foreign policy. It shows Uncle Sam dancing with a uniformed skeleton labeled "War" while a saddened "Peace" stands by. Birds fly over new graves in the background. Many of Walker's cartoons criticized the Spanish-American War and imperialism in general. (Library of Congress)

This cartoon by Keppler and Schartzmann shows Uncle Sam and Lady Liberty at the gates of an orphanage, pondering whether to accept three more foundlings: Cuba, Hawaii and the Phillipines. The strong arms of Manifest Destiny are delivering the basket. (Puck)

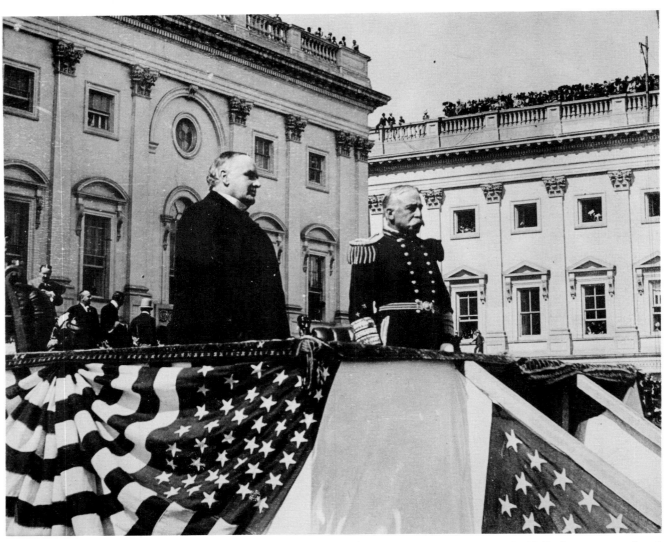

The presentation of the nation's sword to Admiral George Dewey in Washington, D.C.. In his speech, McKinley announced to the admiral, "There was no flaw in your victory; there will be no falter in maintaining it." (Canton *Repository*)

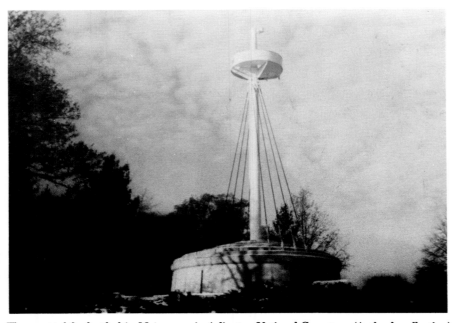

The mast of the battleship *Maine* now in Arlington National Cemetery. (Author's collection)

127

W. McKinley

Pictured here (left) is the shattered base of the *U.S.S. Maine's* conning tower. It was erected in 1912 to honor Stark County's Spanish-American War veterans. Nearby are a large cannon (bottom) and a captured Spanish artillery piece (below). These are located in Water Works Park between West Tuscarawas and Seventh Streets Northwest in Canton, Ohio. (Tim Wedekamm)

CHAPTER IX

MCKINLEY'S AMERICA–A PANORAMA

No chief executive before McKinley had seen so much of his country. As a soldier, student, politician, and campaigner, he traveled the length and breadth of America. He had witnessed profound changes since his boyhood days in Niles. The great forces of invention which took place during the Civil War and the Reconstruction Era and the Gilded Age shaped the temper and quality of American life, enlarging the scope of imagination and creativity.

By the end of McKinley's first term in 1900, the United States' population had reached nearly seventy-eight million. Included in this figure were ten million minority Americans, mostly black and Hispanic, along with a quarter of a million Indians, nearly all confined to reservations. Primarily located in the West were an additional ninety thousand Chinese and twenty-four thousand Japanese. Since the Civil War, the nation had moved from a rural-agrarian society to an urban-industrial one. Toward the end of the nineteenth century, one half of the population lived in cities or large towns.

During the latter half of the 1800s, Americans experienced unparalleled growth characterized by a number of marked achievements and changes in lifestyles. Among these were the advent of the electric light and phonograph,

By 1860 canals and railroads linked most communities in the north and east. Ohio towns such as Canton, Akron, Alliance, and Navarre (where McKinley tried one of his first cases) were prospering and growing. Early canal scene, probably 1860s. (Ohio Historical Society)

Travel by steamboat was fast and inexpensive. There was an alarming rate of accidents and deaths due to boiler explosions and fires. (Smithsonian Institution)

The electric trolley became the mode of transportation in cities during the transition period between the horse and the automobile. (National Archives)

The whaling industry was beginning to diminish in importance by the early 1900s. This picture was taken in Tampa, Florida. (Stark County Historical Society)

McKinley was one of only two presidents between Lincoln and Taft who were clean shaven (Andrew Johnson was the other).

Schooners and commercial ships in Portland, Maine, 1895. Steel ships, powered by steam, soon replaced the wooden ones shown here. Canvas sails on masts gave way to smokestacks. (Detroit Publishing Company)

trolleys which replaced horse-drawn cars, the telephone and typewriter, and the rise of monopolies and labor unions. In what leisure time they had, many Americans attended the theater or watched college football or professional baseball.

At the 1893 Chicago Exposition, the new Ferris wheel took streetcar-sized loads of passengers two hundred feet into the air, while eager men and shocked women saw Little Egypt dance the hootchy-kootchy in a state of near nakedness. People were reading Twain's *Huckleberry Finn*, Ned Buntline's dime novels, Whitman's *Leaves of Grass*, Grant's *Memoirs*, Crane's *Red Badge of Courage*, and even "funnies" in the newspapers. William McGuffey's *Eclectic Reader* for school children helped shape the character of the nation. Divorce was a rarity and few married women worked outside the home. Religion played a major factor in most families, while fathers generally worked ten to twelve hour days.

There were also changes in transportation. Railroads carried more than five-hundred million passengers a year; steamboats dotted the Ohio and Mississippi, while inland canals became less important. More and better roadways were constructed. The automobile, still a curious nuisance to a horse and buggy generation, was just in its infancy. Bold adventurers such as Orville and Wilbur Wright, bicycle repairmen from Dayton, Ohio, were tinkering with the idea of flight, and American ingenuity added mechanical marvels to the world of industry and amusement. Overseas, Röntgen's x-ray machine and Marconi's wireless radio were already in use.

> *McKinley was the last president who served in the Civil War.*

Native Americans resisted the government's "pacification" policy. Indians had no desire to be confined to reservations, and between 1866 and 1880 more than two hundred battles and massacres took place. During the Grant administration, General Philip Sheridan waged war on western tribes. Here a Cheyenne family pitched their summer camp on the Plains (c. 1875). (Library of Congress)

Despite the dangers and inconveniences, settlers trekked west. By 1890 the frontier in the conterminous United States no longer existed. (Denver Public Library)

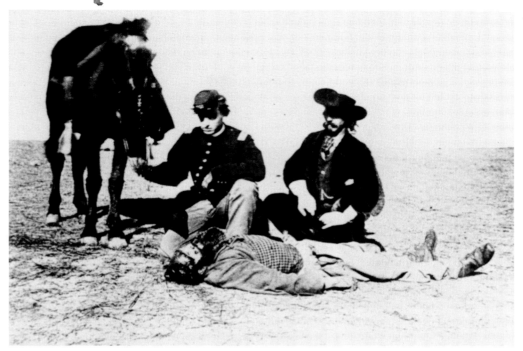

Here a hunter has been killed and scalped by Indians near Fort Dodge, Kansas, in 1869. (Smithsonian Institution)

A scene in the marsh on the Anacostia River in the nation's capital in 1882. (National Archives)

A dozen children pile in this small cart owned by a former slave in Mississippi. (Stark County Historical Society)

Negro sharecroppers in southern Mississippi sharing a meal. (Stark County Historical Society)

Very little changed for most southern Negroes after the Civil War. Poverty, ignorance, and discrimination remained their lot. (Robert Dennis Collection)

Prohibitionists, suffragettes, new religious sects, struggles between labor and capital, the destruction of the buffalo, the rape of land in search of minerals, breakthroughs in medicine and physics, the rise of charitable organizations, and the development of the arts made Americans more aware of their national treasures, dilemmas and paradoxes.

Poverty reached new levels, particularly in the eastern cities. Child labor existed in nearly every state. Racial prejudice was accepted and tolerated. By 1900 there had been hundreds of lynchings in the South, most of the victims black. Few politicians cared to address this problem. Many blacks came north to find work while most in Dixie remained illiterate sharecroppers, their condition little better than before the Civil War when they were enslaved.

By the end of Grover Cleveland's term as the twenty-fourth president, the amount of money in circulation had fallen dramatically and monetary policy centered around whether gold or silver should support the money system. During the McKinley presidency, the output of gold more than doubled compared to the previous administration. Though prices rose in the late 1890s, so did the supply of money as newly mined gold from Alaska flowed into the channels of the American economy. McKinley, favoring sound money based on the gold standard, eventually secured adoption of both gold and silver (bimetallism), envisioning an international agreement to promote silver. McKinley also moved carefully to encourage reduction of the tariffs he had so vigorously promoted as a congressman. Before his death, an Open Door policy promoted extensive trade with China.

Sharecroppers picking cotton near Jackson, Tennessee in the 1880s. (Culver Pictures of New York)

An algebra class at Tuskegee Institute in Alabama. (Library of Congress)

By the turn of the century the gap between rich and poor was startling. Here a mother and daughter live in a New York slum. (Library of Congress)

This smartly dressed couple pose near the south portico of the White House. They are seated on their 1886 model of a bicycle built for two. (National Archives)

Some of New York City's upper "400" at a gala in 1900. McKinley had strong backing from the wealthy as well as from the working class. (Library of Congress)

Child labor existed in mills, factories and mines throughout the nineteenth century in every state. Children working in coal mines, pictured here, often led to disastrous results. (National Archives)

Youngsters working in a sweatshop at the turn of the century. Reformers made the public aware of the abuses of child labor. As governor of Ohio, McKinley sought to abolish such conditions for children. (Library of Congress)

Leather workers proudly display their horse collars (stacked at the left) in this 1888 picture of Will Hoover's small company, later to become the Hoover Vacuum Company in New Berlin (North Canton), Ohio. Hoover is seated fourth from the left. (Hoover Historical Center)

Many Americans demanded restricting Chinese immigration. These coolies pictured here worked on building a railroad in Deadwood, South Dakota, in 1888. (Library of Congress)

The horse-drawn fire engine always attracted a great deal of excitement. (National Archives and Brown Brothers)

This cartoon was published in the *New York Journal* in 1899, at a time when few people believed the horse would be replaced. (New York Journal)

The horse and buggy were giving way to the automobile. This photo was taken in Vermont in 1900. McKinley became the first incumbent president to ride in a horseless carriage. (Vermont Historical Society)

The barbershop was exclusively a man's world. This one was pictured in 1900 in Junction City, Kansas. (Pennell Collection, University of Kansas)

A drugstore owner and his employees in Springfield, Massachusetts, before the turn of the century. This photograph was taken by Alvah and George Howes. (Library of Congress)

A family outing near Columbus, Ohio, in 1897. (Ohio Historical Society)

The tall trees of the northwest were being harvested at a rapid rate, drawing the attention of conservationists. These lumberjacks posed for Darius Kinsey and his wife, who owned a photography studio near Seattle. (Library of Congress)

139

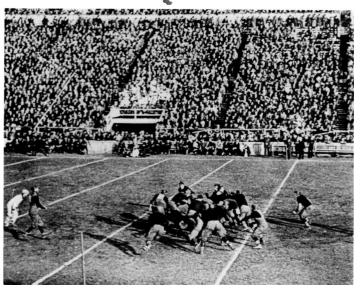

In 1890 McKinley, as a guest of Mark Hanna, attended his first collegiate football game (Yale v. Princeton). (National Archives and T.S. Bronson)

Basketball was in its infancy. This is a photo of the 1900-01 team at Lombard University in Galesburg, Illinois. The man holding the ball is the team captain, Carl Sandburg. (Knox College)

McKinley was an avid baseball fan, supporting the teams in Canton and Columbus during his terms as congressman and governor. This picture was taken in the mid-1880s. (Ohio Historical Society)

W. D. Smith, captain of the West Point football team, 1899. (*Collier's* Weekly)

G. G. Hubbard of Harvard was one of the best amateur golfers in 1899. (*Collier's* Weekly)

> *In an 1896 speech to students at Mount Union College in Alliance, Ohio, William McKinley reminded them that too much education was not necessarily a guarantee for success. He warned them, "Do not permit college ideals to warp you."*

Elementary school children and their teacher at the turn of the century. (Library of Congress)

(above) George Ferris' Wheel at the Chicago Columbian Exposition (also known as the World's Fair) in 1893. It could hold more than twenty-one hundred passengers at one time. McKinley attended the World's Fair to dedicate Ohio Day and attend a McKinley family reunion. (Library of Congress)

Among the many rides offered at the Chicago World's Fair was a camel. (National Archives)

After McKinley became president the nation began to emerge from a depression. Although he recognized the evils of monopoly, McKinley believed it necessary to first restore prosperity through the growth of big business. The concentration of capital was well established by 1890, and McKinley treaded lightly in curbing this power because many wealthy businessmen supported his candidacy. But this changed near the end of his first term when he publicly attacked the big trusts. Early on, he favored restriction of immigration "when our laboring people are in such distress." These restrictions were eased during the last two years of his administration. ▨

Oil rig in the Kern River District, California, in 1898. (National Archives)

On October 7, 1898, Ida McKinley's brother George Saxton, age forty-nine, was found shot to death near the front steps of the home of widow Eva Althouse in Canton, Ohio. A female figure, dressed in black, hid behind some bushes and fired the fatal shots; she was identified as Annie George. She and George Saxton had had a fifteen year affair, though Annie was married with two sons. George paid for her divorce and there followed a series of lawsuits between them for the next six years as the affair cooled. Annie demanded money for living expenses and when she did not receive it, she sent threatening letters. George found a new lady friend, and on that fateful October day he had ridden his bicycle over to Eva's house wearing a flower and carrying three cigars and a bottle of champagne. News of the shooting understandably shocked the first family even though they and everyone else in Canton knew George was a frivolous playboy who squandered his money. A curious nation awaited the trial of Annie George, which lasted for three weeks in 1899. She denied the first degree murder charge and refused to answer questions by the prosecutor. However, public sentiment for Annie, a sympathetic jury, and the lack of conclusive evidence led to her acquittal to the cheers of a crowd of spectators. In 1902 Annie was still working in a dressmaker's shop in Canton. Soon thereafter she and her sons left town never to be heard from again.

The gold rush in the Yukon not only brought hundreds of prospectors to Alaska and northwestern Canada, but thousands of others as well. Surveying teams from the United States government, like the one pictured here, laid out boundaries. This D.L.Brainard photograph was captioned "Scales and Summit of Chilkoot Pass, 1898."(National Archives)

(above) One of the few remaining Reconstruction-era blacks in Congress after 1890, Henry P. Cheatham of North Carolina served in the House of Representatives with McKinley. Later, Cheatham was appointed as registrar of deeds for the District of Columbia by President McKinley. (Author's collection)

(left) Queen Liliuokalani of Hawaii tried to increase her powers limited by a constitution. In 1893 the queen was deposed when a bloodless revolution, encouraged by American business executives led by Sanford Dole, established a republic. (Stark County Historical Society)

In the foreground, left to right, are General Horace Porter, President McKinley, Lord Julian Pauncefote, and Vice-President Hobart. They are attending the dedication of Grant's Monument in Philadelphia on April 27, 1899. McKinley remarked in his speech that Grant was "a typical American, free from ostentation...a man from the people, for the people, and never above the people." (*Frank Leslie's Weekly*)

Wealthy sugar planters succeeded in annexing Hawaii to the United States. McKinley appointed Dole as the first governor. The president could not attend the official ceremonies, pictured here, in Honolulu on August 12, 1898. (Stark County Historical Society)

A bust of John G. Battelle, a devoted and loyal friend of McKinley. Battelle made the first sheet of tin plate in the United States, established the tin plate industry, and founded the Battelle Institute. He died in Columbus in 1918. (National McKinley Birthplace Memorial)

McKinley loved children, as evidenced by this picture of his visit to Carleton, Michigan. (*Harper's Weekly*)

The Plunketts of Adams, Massachusetts, were close friends of the McKinleys and visited each other often. In 1899 McKinley attended his niece Grace's graduation from Mt. Holyoke, then went to commencement exercises at Smith College. McKinley also laid a cornerstone for one of Plunkett's new buildings at his cotton manufacturing plant. The families pose for a picture at the Plunkett's home. (Stark County Historical Society)

McKinley poses with Florida's Governor William Bloxham in 1899. Ida sits directly behind him, between Mrs. Hanna and Mrs. Bloxham. Mark Hanna is standing behind Ida. (Stark County Historical Society)

McKinley made a genuine effort to bridge the gap between races. Here he stands between Alabama Governor Joseph F. Johnston and Booker T. Washington at Tuskeegee Institute. (Stark County Historical Society)

Critics of the McKinley administration may not have believed the president when, at a New York City speech on March 3, 1900, he told an audience, "There can be no imperialism...No imperial designs lurk in the American mind."

McKinley being welcomed by Tuskeegee's mayor, 1899. (Stark County Historical Society)

The president returns the salutes of passing ships at the New Orleans River Parade in 1901. (Stark County Historical Society)

As the Texas wind tosses his hair, McKinley meets with children in El Paso. General Hernandez of Mexico, representing President Porifirio Diaz, stands on the right. (*Harper's Weekly*)

The school children of El Paso honor McKinley. (Stark County Historical Society)

The same parade. (Stark County Historical Society)

The president enters his carriage in El Paso, carrying the flag of the Texas Republic. (Stark County Historical Society)

At Des Moines, Iowa, McKinley posed with his nieces and cabinet members' wives. (Stark County Historical Society)

President McKinley, Secretary of State Hay and Postmaster-General Smith at a mine near Phoenix, Arizona. (Canton *Repository*)

(far left) On his transcontinental trip in 1901, President McKinley made many stops. In this picture the presidential party, excluding the McKinleys, is about to descend a three thousand foot gold mine shaft near Phoenix. (Stark County Historical Society)

(left) A miner's daughter asks the president to pose for a picture. (*Harper's Weekly*)

McKinley addresses a large crowd in San Jose, California. (Canton *Repository*)

McKinley at a stop in California in May of 1901. Secret Service Agent and body guard George E. Foster stands at the right. (Stark County Historical Society)

Visiting San Francisco Bay. (Stark County Historical Society)

The Chinese Celestial Dragon passed before the president in Los Angeles. (Stark County Historical Society)

The honored guest, at the extreme right, watches the Los Angeles parade from a reviewing stand. (Stark County Historical Society)

A group of Rough Riders salute their commander-in-chief at a Los Angeles parade. (Stark County Historical Society)

On May 30, 1900, President McKinley attended a dedication at the battlefield of Antietam in Sharpsburg, Maryland. One comment in his speech reminded the listeners, "American soldiers never surrendered but to Americans."

The presidential Tally-ho party at San Francisco's Golden Gate Park. At the time Ida was seriously ill from a blood infection, recovering in a San Francisco hotel. (*Collier's* Magazine)

The decorated presidential train leaving Oakland, California. (Stark County Historical Society)

CHAPTER X

APPOINTMENT WITH DEATH

On New Year's Day of 1901 the McKinleys opened the White House to the public. Ida appeared refreshed, greeting visitors, chatting lively and kissing children. More than fifty-four hundred callers were ushered past the president, who stood next to his seated wife. Shaking hands for nearly three hours could be taxing, especially on Ida who was often fatigued or ill. She took a gentle swipe at her husband when she later remarked in her diary, "My Dearest was tired out."

An era ended a few days later when the world learned Queen Victoria had died . The president sent his personal sympathies, but he too fell ill. This news was kept secret from the press and on Valentine's Day the McKinleys hosted a dance for invited guests. The Marine band played a variety of tunes including waltzes and even ragtime. At the annual Gridiron Club dinner on March 27 the president was "roasted" and entertained by some vaudeville tunes, then presented with a pie six feet in diameter.

In the spring McKinley readied for a grand tour around the country. This swing through the South and West, by train, was to serve several purposes. At every stop McKinley spoke to large crowds, **attacking the Senate's opposition to any expansion of trade. There were**

A program from the Pan-American Exposition. (Stark County Historical Society)

151

The McKinleys in Buffalo, September 5, 1901. (Canton *Repository*)

Booming guns heralded the arrival of the president and first lady in Buffalo. The noise was too much for Ida and she fainted. In this photograph Dr. Rixey accompanies Mrs. McKinley while Secret Service agent Foster trails them. (Canton *Repository*)

seven trade agreements stalled in the monopoly-controlled Senate, and the president was furious. He wanted to rally public support, and he did not hesitate mentioning the abuses of the business trusts, most of which had backed him in both elections. The main theme of his speeches, however, was patriotic and uplifting in context.

McKinley was also scheduled to christen the new battleship *Ohio*, built in Oakland, California. In addition, he planned to visit old friends, attend parades, and speak to tens of thousands of school children. On April 29 he and Ida left Washington with forty-three others, including two nieces. The trip was to end in June with a final stop at the Pan American Exposition in Buffalo, New York.

By the time the party reached El Paso, Ida was not feeling well. During the second week of May she had an infected index finger lanced by Dr. Presley Rixey, the president's personal physician. She ran a high fever, developed a severe case of diarrhea, and reinfected her finger, which was lanced a second time. By the time the train reached the San Francisco-Oakland area, Ida was seriously ill and was confined to bed for a week with around-the-clock nurses. By now Dr. Rixey realized the first lady had a serious blood infection. Ida's health deteriorated so much that a cable was sent to the White House suggesting funeral arrangements be made. In spite of these setbacks, the president kept to his busy schedule. Reporters commented that the crowds were deeply moved by the news of his wife's condition. Ida regained her strength, but the trip was cut short as the train headed back to Washington. In July, the couple returned to Canton for some much needed rest and relaxation. Their appearance at the Buffalo Exposition was postponed until September. Just before the trip, Ida wrote in her diary, "I wish

McKinley enjoyed a carriage ride in Rainbow City at the Exposition grounds in Buffalo. Notice the Temple of Music building in the background to the left. He was shot there the next day. (Stark County Historical Society)

Exposition officials in Buffalo had been told Mrs. McKinley did not enjoy loud noises, especially those made by cannons. As the McKinley train, The Presidential Special, pulled into Terrace Station in Buffalo, a twenty-one gun salute greeted the president and first lady. The blasts were so powerful that eight windows in one of the passenger cars blew out. The train shook and two passengers were knocked to the floor of the baggage car. Windows in nearby buildings shattered and glass fell to the pavement. Though Mrs. McKinley fainted (revived by Dr. Rixey), the president emerged and waved to the crowd.

The Exposition grounds at night, with the Temple of Music on the left. (Roy W. Nagle collection)

McKinley made out his will in 1897, leaving most of his estate to his wife Ida. He further decreed that his estate be divided among his brothers and sisters following the death of Ida. This caused a controversy over the share willed to his brother Abner, who died after William but before the estate was settled. The executors of Abner's estate sued to recover his share, but lost the suit.

On September 5, 1901, McKinley took a tour of Niagara Falls. He met Ida at the International Hotel where they had lunch. *(Frank Leslie's Weekly)*

(Canton *Repository*)

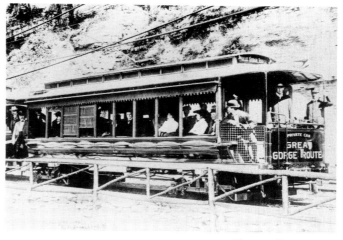

(Canton *Repository*)

These three pictures show McKinley on his Niagara Falls visit. The large crowds and stifling heat may have given him second thoughts. During the sightseeing he remarked, "I don't know whether I'll ever be able to get away from Buffalo."

(Stark County Historical Society)

McKinley with his secretary of interior and ardent conservationist Ethan Hitchcock (left) and Exposition President John Milburn at the Falls. Standing behind them is Secret Service Agent Foster. (Canton *Repository*)

The president being escorted by Brigadier General Welch at the stadium in Buffalo. September 5 was designated President's Day and McKinley gave his last public speech to an estimated crowd of fifty thousand. (Canton *Repository*)

The president's last speech. (*Frank Leslie's Weekly*)

On September 5, 1901, President McKinley strode through the Exposition stadium, escorted by General Samuel Welch. Thousands cheered as McKinley walked past mounted troops, then headed for the stands. At this point the United States Marine mascot, Billy Goat Marine, broke ranks and headed right towards the president. The crowd roared with laughter as Billy stopped in front of McKinley, who smiled and waved to acknowledge the goat's welcome. McKinley stayed only five minutes before leaving to visit some exhibits.

The president leaves the International Hotel, September 6. (Stark County Historical Society)

we were not going away from home."

The Buffalo itinerary called for a public reception at the Exposition's Temple of Music where McKinley would greet the people. White House secretary George Cortelyou twice removed this visit from the list, and twice it was put back at the insistence of the president. Cortelyou, fearing for McKinley's safety, appealed to his boss to forego the reception. McKinley explained that he had no enemies and there was nothing to fear.

Just when Leon Czolgosz decided to shoot McKinley is not known. It is possible, even likely, that he stalked the president for several weeks prior to the assassination at the Buffalo Exposition.

The assassin was a devoted follower of Emma Goldman, the leading anarchist speaker at the time. Goldman was a Russian revolutionary who came to the United States in 1885. In America she joined a group of anarchists who opposed all forms of government. She led a number of crusades and had served time in prison for advocating anarchy, birth control, and women's rights. Goldman lectured throughout the East and Midwest, appealing to the oppressed people to protest or use violence to achieve their goals. Although her views mellowed somewhat after McKinley's death, she was deported after the end of World War I.

Several monarchs, including the Shah of Persia and the Tsar of Russia, had been assassinated in the late 1800s. Police departments in France and England informed American officials in the spring of 1901 that a steady stream of anarchists was bound for the United States. Secretary Cortelyou became quite concerned and took steps to

McKinley's arrival at the Exposition on the day of the shooting. (Stark County Historical Society)

This picture was taken a short time before the shooting on September 6. McKinley attended a reception in the Mission Building and posed with, Joseph Brigham, his very tall assistant secretary of agriculture. (Canton *Repository*)

One of several photos taken just before entering the Temple of Music. (Stark County Historical Society)

The Temple of Music building. (Stark County Historical Society)

The crowd waiting in line in front of the Temple of Music. It was announced the president would shake hands after the people were ushered in. The assassin was among the first to enter. (*Frank Leslie's Weekly*)

President McKinley smoked his final Garcia cigar at 3:50 p.m., just fifteen minutes before he was shot. After visiting the Mission Building, he stopped for a quick smoke and a cup of chocolate on his way to the Temple of Music.

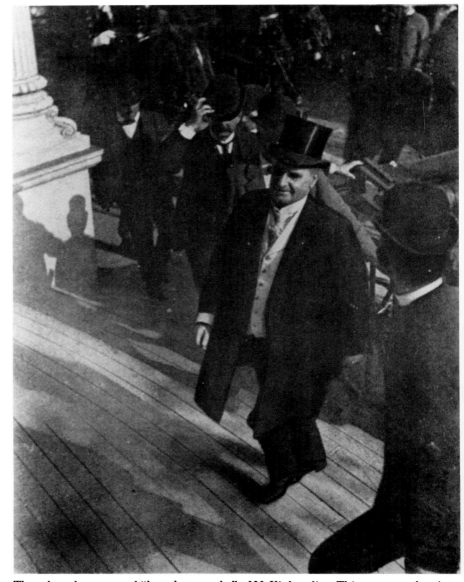

There have been several "last photographs" of McKinley alive. This one was taken just before he entered the Temple of Music building where he was shot. (Canton *Repository*)

provide more protection for his boss. Mark Hanna expressed fear that McKinley would not live out a second term.

Czolgosz was born in Detroit to Polish parents. He left school and worked as a blacksmith's apprentice before moving to Cleveland and later, Chicago. Drifting back and forth among cities in the Midwest, he took on a number of odd jobs and attended socialist meetings. He heard a speech by Goldman and was captivated. Czolgosz agreed with Goldman in denouncing American expansionist policy which had cost the lives of Americans, Cubans, and Filipinos. Something, he believed, should be done.

In 1898 Czolgosz moved back to his family's farm near Cleveland. Having suffered a nervous breakdown, he became increasingly irritable and reclusive. He purchased a five-shot .32 caliber Iver Johnson revolver for three dollars and ten cents, ordering it from a Sears and Roebuck catalogue.

Evidence shows Czolgosz may have tried to kill McKinley in Canton. According to the testimony of William Arntz, an employee at Meyers Lake Park in Canton, the assassin was there in the early summer of 1901. Arntz recalled he knew McKinley and his wife, who came to the park "in a surrey and sat on the grass on the hillside in the picnic area and watched the crowd. There was a shooting gallery on the grounds where the Canton Gun Club allowed members to try their luck at hitting clay pigeons, but 'No Firearms Allowed Here.' were posted."

Arntz further explained, "One day while I was gathering the clay pigeons that all the shooters missed, I saw a man who had two guns strapped on, walking along in the picnic area. When I reminded the

Two sketches of the shooting. The one showing the hatless assassin is the most accurate. (*Judge* magazine and Stark County Historical Society)

Agents Ireland (left) and Foster who accompanied McKinley in Buffalo. (*Judge* magazine)

man that firearms were not allowed on the grounds, the man, whom I later learned was Leon Czolgosz, replied, 'I don't pay any attention to things like that,' and strode on with a handful of pink flowers. I whistled for the police. Czolgosz took off and they never did find him nor did anyone figure out how he got away. They never did find Czolgosz until he got to Buffalo and shot President McKinley."

Czolgosz headed for Buffalo where he rented a two-dollar-a-week room at John Nowak's saloon. Czolgosz made a number of attempts to get near McKinley in Buffalo. During McKinley's last speech on September 5, Czolgosz stood in the front row of the crowd but apparently lost his nerve to shoot. After the speech, he followed the president to his carriage and tried to get close but a guard caught him by the shoulder and shoved him back. He then followed the president to the stadium, but guards would not allow him to pass through the main entrance.

The next day, Friday, September 6, Czolgosz stood at the doors of the Temple of Music. McKinley was ushered in through a side door and, once inside announced he wanted to meet the people who were standing and waiting outside. Czolgosz was one of the first to enter as the crowd pressed forward to the stage where McKinley stood ready to shake hands. Rather than try to conceal a pistol which might arouse suspicion, Czolgosz put it inside

Newspaper sketch showing assassin Leon Czolgosz pinioned by officers and guards while waiting for the police. (Stark County Historical Society)

James B. Parker. A man of Spanish-Negro descent, Parker grabbed Czolgosz and prevented him from firing a third shot. (*Frank Leslie's Weekly*)

his bandaged right hand and held it close to his chest.

McKinley knew how to move a crowd along quickly. His routine of grasping an extended arm, gently squeezing the hand, then guiding it past him as he turned to the next person in line allowed him to meet thousands of people at various functions. As the orchestra played a Bach sonata, people were led to the president, surrounded by many police officers and guards. A breakdown in regulations occurred when the guards did not enforce the rule that any person walking towards the president must have both hands clearly visible and empty.

McKinley's coordinated effort of handshaking was interrupted when twelve-year-old Myrtle Ledger of Springbrook, New York, accompanied by her mother, asked if she could have the red carnation the president was wearing. Rarely did he remove the flower, believing it to be a good omen. Nevertheless, he unpinned his good luck charm and gave it to the girl.

The agents and guards assigned to protect McKinley grew a bit worried when they spotted a man who looked suspicious. He was short, dark complexioned, dressed in a dark suit, and appeared restless. Secret Service Agents Foster, Ireland, and Gallaher all breathed a sigh of relief after McKinley shook this man's hand without incident. Behind this fellow, however, was a tall, twenty-six year old well-dressed man with handsome features, and an apparently injured hand. It was 4:07 p.m.

Seeing Czolgosz with a bandaged right hand, McKinley reached to shake the man's left hand. Just as their fingers touched, two quick shots rang out. For a brief moment McKinley lurched forward on his

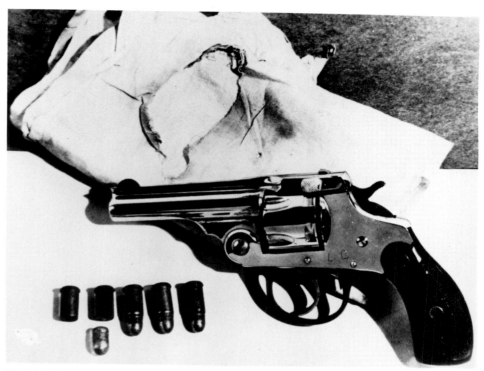

The .32 caliber pistol and handkerchief taken from the assassin. Only one of the bullets was recovered. The other one was still in McKinley's body. More than sixty guards, including a dozen inexperienced and unarmed soldiers, were positioned inside the building. Secretary George Cortelyou had insisted McKinley greet the people for only ten minutes—and no more. The doors were opened at 4:00 p.m. and Cortelyou clasped his watch. At precisely 4:07 Czolgosz confirmed Cortelyou's worst fears. (Buffalo and Erie County Historical Society)

This picture was taken just after the shooting. McKinley stood in front of and between the potted trees. (Buffalo and Erie County Historical Society)

toes as gun smoke swirled between him and the assailant. Before a third shot could be fired, John Parker, a six foot one inch black man from Georgia, and a nearby marine both grabbed the revolver. As the president fell backwards to the right, others wrestled Czolgosz to the floor. McKinley asked that the assassin not be harmed, later referring to him as some "misguided fellow." Leaning on his escorts, the president was taken to a chair, tripping over some flag bunting which had been trampled in the chaos. At this point McKinley turned to his secretary and said, "Cortelyou, my wife! Oh, be careful how you tell her." Not wanting to see the assassin harmed, McKinley, according to newspapers, said, "Let no one harm him." What he actually said was, "Be easy with him, boys."

The doors of the Temple were closed and an electric motor car ambulance was summoned. Taken to a small emergency hospital at the

This electric ambulance took McKinley from the Temple of Music to a small infirmary at the Exposition where emergency surgery was performed. (Stark County Historical Society)

A multitude waits at the emergency hospital during the operation on McKinley. (Buffalo News Company)

These two nurses, Miss Simmons and Miss Barnes, attended the wounded president at the emergency hospital and at the Milburn house. (*Judge* Company and *Frank Leslie's Weekly*)

The home of John Milburn. (Library of Congress)

fairgrounds, McKinley was examined by a pair of doctors. The first shot had struck his breastbone but had been deflected, most likely by a shirt or coat button. The second bullet, however, pierced his stomach. Dr. Matthew Mann, an obstetrician, decided immediate surgery was necessary. McKinley was given an injection of morphine to ease his pain. Before ether was administered he recited the Lord's Prayer.

Dr. Rixey and Dr. Herman Mynter soon arrived and assisted in a difficult operation in dim light. Though lacking proper facilities in the small infirmary, the doctors spent an hour and twenty minutes in surgery, discovering that the bullet had passed through the front and rear walls of the stomach. They could not locate the .32 caliber bullet, and when McKinley's pulse rate began to increase, they sutured the stomach wounds. Dr. Roswell Park, a leading expert in abdominal surgery, arrived just as the operation was ending. Understandably, he was hesitant to interfere and at 5:20 p.m. McKinley was given another injection of morphine and allowed to waken.

Following his emergency operation, the president was taken by the electric ambulance to the home of John Milburn, president of the Exposition. His house became a temporary hospital as relatives rushed to Buffalo. McKinley's requests for a cigar were denied and while his condition fluctuated over the next several days, he was subjected to many enemas and injections of different medicines including morphine, digitalis, saline solutions, camphorated oil, strychnine, and a new drug called adrenaline. The fourth day after the shooting, minor surgery was performed to remove a small

---

Minutes after President McKinley was shot at the Pan American Exposition in Buffalo in 1901, he was taken to a small emergency hospital nearby. He was escorted by Dr. Matthew Mann and Dr. Presley Rixey, his personal physician. As the wound was being examined, Dr. Herman Mynter entered. McKinley, who possessed a rare gift for remembering names, recalled meeting Mynter the day before. He said, "Doctor, when I met you yesterday, I did not imagine that today I should have to ask a favor of you." Mynter expressed surprise that McKinley remembered him after greeting thousands of others. Dr. Mann, in the meantime, had already decided surgery was necessary in order to find the bullet deep in McKinley's abdomen. McKinley had no way of knowing that Dr. Mann was an obstetrician/gynecologist who had never operated on a male patient nor treated a gunshot wound. The three physicians, led by Dr. Mann, could not locate the bullet. The incisions were sutured and the patient was sent to John Milburn's house where he died eight days later.

McKinley was taken to the house of John Milburn in Buffalo. Pictured here are McKinley's sisters, Miss Helen McKinley (in front) and Mrs. Sarah Duncan, with her husband, leaving the Milburn house. (*Collier's* magazine)

Abner McKinley, the president's brother, and his wife, after visiting the Milburn home. Abner was in Colorado at the time of the shooting and hurried by train to Buffalo. Relatives were told McKinley's condition was improving. (*Collier's* magazine)

Only a very few visitors were allowed to see McKinley. Mark Hanna, with cane, was among them. (*Judge* magazine)

McKinley's personal secretary, George B. Cortelyou. (Stark County Historical Society)

A delegation of seven hundred Native Americans, led by Geronimo (left) and Chief Red Cloud, was scheduled to meet with McKinley. (National Archives)

fragment of clothing the bullet had carried into the abdomen.

News bulletins sounded optimistic. Vice-President Roosevelt, vacationing with his family in the Adirondack Mountains near the New York-Vermont border, arrived by special train but left after a short visit when doctors reassured him McKinley would recover. The bullet, however, remained undiscovered. Thomas Edison telegraphed to say they could use his new x-ray machine, on display at the Exposition, to locate the bullet. The doctors, seeing some improvement in their patient, and not wanting to move him, declined the offer.

The wound was treated with antiseptic and the dressing was changed three times a day. McKinley's food consisted mostly of beef broth while solid food was withheld since he could not digest it. His pulse rate showed danger signs and he continued to receive regular daily enemas.

The president was dying. Gangrene was spreading even as several attending physicians congratulated themselves for saving his life. Dr. Park, however, was one of the few who feared the worst. A week after he was shot, McKinley told his doctors, "It is useless, gentlemen. I think we ought to have prayer." Ida was summoned and told her husband that she wanted to go too. She held his hand as he began to sink. He told her, "It is God's way. His will, not ours, be done." The first lady was led away never to see her husband alive again. The twenty-fifth chief executive died at 2:15 a.m. on Saturday morning, September 14, 1901. Theodore Roosevelt, hurrying from his mountain retreat, arrived after McKinley's death and was immediately sworn in as president.

Dr. P. M. Rixey, the McKinley family physician, who along with a team of other doctors, looked after the president. (*Judge* magazine)

Miss Grace MacKenzie, the Philadelphia nurse who attended the president during his last hours. (*Judge* magazine)

Cortelyou meets with reporters to give them an update on the president's condition. (*Judge* magazine)

Anxious noon day crowds like this one pictured here in New York City, gathered for news bulletins of McKinley's condition. (Library of Congress)

This flashlight photo was taken of reporters and others as they appeared outside the Milburn house at 2:20 a.m. just after McKinley's death was announced. (*Judge* Company and *Frank Leslie's Weekly*)

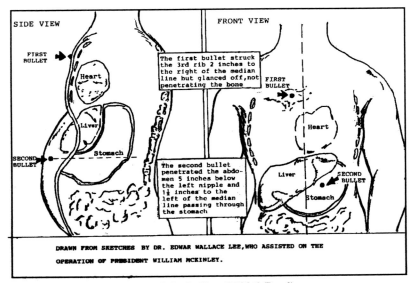

SIDE VIEW   FRONT VIEW

FIRST BULLET

Heart

The first bullet struck the 3rd rib 2 inches to the right of the median line but glanced off, not penetrating the bone

FIRST BULLET

Liver

Heart

Stomach

SECOND BULLET

The second bullet penetrated the abdomen 5 inches below the left nipple and 1½ inches to the left of the median line passing through the stomach

Liver

SECOND BULLET

Stomach

DRAWN FROM SKETCHES BY DR. EDWAR WALLACE LEE, WHO ASSISTED ON THE OPERATION OF PRESIDENT WILLIAM MCKINLEY.

Diagram showing the path of the bullet. (Nikhil Patel)

An autopsy was performed. For nearly three hours Dr. Mann and a team of thirteen other physicians examined the wound and looked for the bullet. Dr. Mynter explained that the bullet "passed first through the abdomen, then through the front and back of the colon transversum, notched off a corner of the left kidney and passed through the rear wall of the peritoneum. After that it disappeared in the muscles of the back..."

The post mortem examination showed that the adrenal gland and pancreas were damaged as well. There was also a degeneration of the heart muscle, and a "brown atrophy" of the fatty tissue around it. Mrs. McKinley requested the autopsy end. The bullet which had led to gangrene poisoning was never found. After a plaster death mask was made, private ceremonies were held in the Milburn home before the body was moved to Buffalo's City Hall.

In hindsight, particularly after advances were made in medical science, an argument can be made that the president did not receive the best of treatment. Post-operatively, McKinley was given almost no nutrients or vitamins. Perhaps if Dr. Park had been in charge of surgery and patient care, things may have turned out quite differently. Certainly, if McKinley had been shot today, his chances of recovery would have been good.

Steady rains failed to discourage ninety thousand people from paying their respects at Buffalo. Among the mourners were seven hundred native Americans who had planned to meet with the "Great White Chief." The leaders of this Indian Congress issued an official statement which read in part, "The rainbow is out of the sky. Heavy clouds hang about us. Tears wet the

W. McKinley

CLEVELAND PLAIN DEALER.

One Cent

SIXTIETH YEAR.   CLEVELAND, SATURDAY MORNING, SEPTEMBER 14, 1901.   Price   NO. 257.

THE PRESIDENT IS DEAD!

After a Day and Night of Brave Battling for Life He Passed Away at 2:15 A. M., His Last Words Being, "It is God's Way; His Will is Done."

He is Dead, but His Words Will Live.

"Our earnest prayer is that God will graciously vouchsafe prosperity, happiness and peace to all our neighbors, and like blessings to all the peoples and powers of earth." The closing words of President McKinley's speech on the day previous to his assassination.

Last Farewells Were Said and the President Lapsed Into Oblivion Murmuring a Hymn.

During His Last Conscious Moments He Had a Pathetic Interview With His Wife.

For Hours He Lay Unconscious and Towards the Last Begged the Doctors to Let Him Die.

BUFFALO, N. Y., Sept. 14.—President McKinley died at 2:15 this morning.

He had been unconscious since 7:50 p. m. His last conscious hour on earth was spent with the wife to whom he devoted a life-time of care. He died unattended by a minister of the gospel, but his last words were a humble submission to the will of the God in whom he believed.

He was reconciled to the cruel fate to which an assassin's bullet had condemned him and faced death in the same spirit of calmness and poise which has marked his long and honorable career. His last conscious words reduced to writing by Dr. Mann, who stood at the bedside, when they were uttered were as follows:

"Goodbye. All goodbye. It is God's way. His will be done."

His relatives, and the members of his official family were at the Milburn house, except Secretary Wilson who did not avail himself of the opportunity and some of his personal and political friends took leave of him.

This painful ceremony was simple. His friends came to the door of the sick room, took a longing glance at him and turned tearfully away.

He was practically unconscious during this time. But the powerful heart stimulants, including oxygen, were employed to restore him to consciousness for his final parting with his wife. He asked for her and she sat at his side and held his hand. He consoled her and bid her goodbye. She went through the heart trying scene with the same bravery and fortitude with which she has borne the grief of the tragedy which ended his life.

The immediate cause of the president's death is undecided. It will possibly require an autopsy to fix the exact cause. The president's remains will be taken to Washington.

Vice President Roosevelt, who now succeeds to the presidency, may take the oath of office wherever he happens to hear the news. The cabinet will of course resign in a body and President Roosevelt will have an opportunity of forming a new cabinet if he so desires.

The rage of the people of Buffalo against the president's assassin when they learned tonight that he was dying was boundless. Thousands surrounded the jail and the entire police force of the city and several companies of militia were utilised to insure his protection.

LAST HOURS OF THE DYING PRESIDENT.

In His Last Hours of Consciousness He Repeated the Words of a Hymn and Bade Farewell to His Wife and Members of His Cabinet.

CROWDS MADE A RUSH FOR THE JAIL.

City Went Into a State of Ferment When the News of the President's Collapse Was Known.

IN HOWISON'S PLACE.

Rear Admiral Ramsay Selected to Sit on the Dobby Court of Inquiry.

ROOSEVELT HEARS THE GRAVE NEWS.

Tidings of the President's Approaching Death Reach Him at a Hunting Camp.

He Starts Immediately for Buffalo but Cannot Reach a Railroad Till This Morning.

Morning edition of the Plain Dealer. McKinley died at 2:15 a.m. on Saturday, September 14, 1901. (Cleveland *Plain Dealer*)

166

Many newspapers, including *Harper's Weekly*, published this sketch mourning the death of McKinley. It was captioned "Entering the Hall of Martyrs." (*Frank Leslie's Weekly*)

McKinley's last act as president concerned instructions given to Secretary of State John Hay regarding negotiations with foreign powers still stationed in China following the Boxer Rebellion.

On his death bed, William McKinley remarked to his secretary George Cortelyou, "It's mighty lonesome in here."

ground of the teepees.....Farewell!"

From Buffalo the remains were taken to the White House where, on the evening of September 15, the body lay without public ceremony. The next day the casket was moved to the Capitol rotunda where many of the one hundred thousand citizens waited for hours in the rain before filing past the open casket. Ida attended these ceremonies but could not go on. She rode the funeral train back to Canton, then withdrew as the nation mourned.

The president's body arrived in Canton on September 18 under partly sunny skies. It laid in state at the Stark County Courthouse where a huge throng, equal to that in Washington, viewed the remains. The next day a special memorial service was held in the First Methodist Church. The casket was closed and sealed, then taken back to the home on North Market Street where relatives paid their final respects. William McKinley was laid to rest in a temporary receiving vault at Westlawn Cemetery.

America's grief was genuine. Not since the death of James A. Garfield in 1881 had it witnessed such a loss. Leaders from nearly every nation sent condolences. There was a financial panic on Wall Street. Bells tolled in every hamlet and city throughout the country. Homes and businesses were draped in black. As McKinley's coffin was laid to rest, economic activity in America came to a halt. Telegraph lines remained silent, streetcars and trains stopped running, and workers paused in silent tribute. All telephone service in the nation was stopped. Many Americans recalled the words of historian and philosopher Henry Adams who considered McKinley, "a very great man; perhaps the greatest we have known since the immortal Washington."

Three views of McKinley's death mask, done by E. L. Pausch of New York twenty-nine hours after the president's death. A thin coat of grease was applied to McKinley's face before plaster of paris was used. The procedure took a half hour. (Stark County Historical Society)

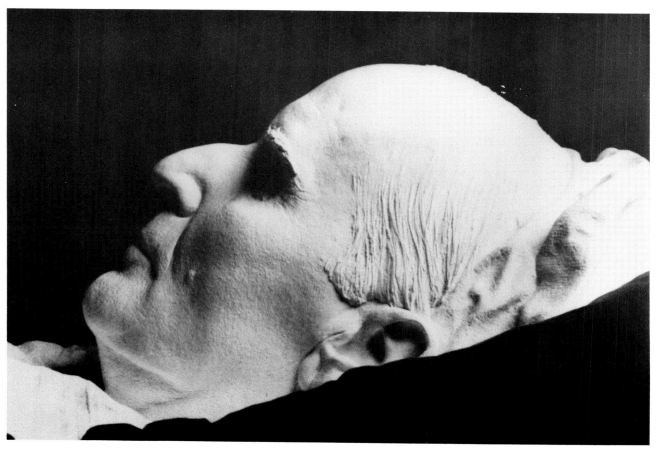

Open casket, lying in state at Buffalo City Hall. (Stark County Historical Society)

Two photographs of McKinley's remains, brought to the White House by soldiers and sailors who stood guard overnight prior to the public funeral service at the Capitol. (*Judge* magazine)

The casket lying in state at the White House. (Stark County Historical Society)

Mourners in the nation's capital waiting to view the body of the twenty-fifth president. (Stark County Historical Society)

McKinley's last words were, "Oh dear." This was whispered to Dr. Presley Rixey just minutes before he died.

Two pictures showing the coffin being taken into the rotunda of the Capitol, September 16, 1901. More than one hundred thousand people paid their respects, filing past the remains. Ida attended the ceremony and accompanied the body back to Canton. (*Frank Leslie's Weekly*)

The funeral procession passing the United States Treasury building. (Canton *Repository*)

The Soldiers Monument on Cleveland's Public Square was draped in black after McKinley's death. As Ohio governor, McKinley had dedicated this memorial in 1894. (Church of The Savior United Methodist of Canton)

Philadelphia's Independence Hall draped in mourning. (*Puck* magazine)

Thousands of mourners watch the McKinley funeral train leave the station in Alliance, Ohio. Flowers were strewn along the tracks as the train heads towards Canton, Ohio. (Stark County Historical Society)

The funeral train pulling into Canton. (Stark County Historical Society)

A color guard in Canton awaits the arrival of the slain leader. (Canton *Repository*)

McKinley's remains being taken from the train in Canton. (Stark County Historical Society)

Funeral procession in Canton, looking east on Tuscarawas Street. (Stark County Historical Society)

This is the Public School Arch on West Tuscarawas Street in front of old Central High School now, the site of Timken High School. (Stark County Historical Society)

Interior of First Methodist Church during memorial services. (Stark County Historical Society)

Crowds entering the Stark County Courthouse to view McKinley's body, September 18. Approximately ninety thousand people witnessed the funeral ceremonies. (Stark County Historical Society)

The courthouse in mourning. (Stark County Historical Society)

Business establishments and entire city blocks were draped in black. This building was across the street from the Stark CountyCourthouse. (Stark County Historical Society)

Canton residents get a last look at the funeral procession. (Stark County Historical Society)

McKinley's funeral cortege passing through Canton. President Theodore Roosevelt's carriage can be seen turning the corner on the right. Movie cameras, on the right, were set up to record the event. (Canton *Repository* and Miss Marguerite K. Reeves)

McKinley funeral procession at square. (Stark County Historical Society)

McKinley made out his last will while he was president. He personally wrote it on two pages.

The Arnold and McCreery Funeral Home borrowed this hearse for the services. It was made in 1901 by Riddle Coach and Hearse Company of Ravenna, Ohio, and was later destroyed by a fire in Cleveland. (Stark County Historical Society)

The hearse during funeral services in Canton. (John L. Arnold and Sons)

Honor Guard at the Westlawn Cemetery receiving vault. (Stark County Historical Society)

The honor guards posted outside the temporary vault, September 19. (Canton *Repository*)

Scenes at Westlawn Cemetery on the day of the funeral. (Stark County Historical Society)

177

Scenes at Westlawn Cemetery on the day of the funeral. (Stark County Historical Society)

178

Encampment of six thousand soldiers at Cook Park in Canton. (Stark County Historical Society)

Soldiers drill just prior to accompanying McKinley's body. (Stark County Historical Society)

One of the floral tributes at Westlawn Cemetery. (Stark County Historical Society)

Secretary of State John Hay addresses Congress to give the eulogy on William McKinley. (Stark County Historical Society)

Interior of the burial vault. (Jim Eakin)

Site of McKinley Memorial Service at the Trinity Cathedral, Tsu-kiji, Tokyo, Japan, September 26, 1901. (National Archives)

Assassin Leon Czolgosz. Police were busy thwarting the many attempts on his life. (*Frank Leslie's Weekly*)

Czolgosz with his lawyers at the trial. (*Judge* magazine)

Hundreds of communists and anarchists were arrested after McKinley's death. This is Emma Goldman, who inspired Leon Czolgosz to adopt the anarchist philosophy. Emigrating from Russia in 1885, she served three separate prison terms while living in the United States. More than once, Emma Goldman had told an audience, "If the life of a tyrant is in your way, take it. The world will applaud your act." After World War I she was deported back to Russia for opposing the draft. (McKinley National Birthplace Memorial)

Czolgosz behind bars. He was the first prisoner in the state of New York executed by alternating current in the electric chair. (Library of Congress)

Great measures were taken to protect the assassin. The crowd outside the Temple of Music, upon learning of the shooting, unleashed its fury after McKinley was taken to the emergency hospital. A hundred or more rushed the building shouting, "Kill him!" and "Hang the bastard!" More people poured forward, pounding on the doors and outside walls until the building shook. Marines and a unit of Coast Guard artillerymen met the mob with loaded rifles and drove it back. Czolgosz remained closely guarded inside, but when he was put in a carriage headed for the Buffalo police station, bystanders followed trying to tear off the fenders and overturn the vehicle. Just as the carriage seemed to break away, men on bicycles chased it until they could no longer stay close. Later, a mob marched to the police station, intent on lynching Czolgosz, but a cordon of mounted police and National Guardsmen used force to disperse the crowd. Though several civilians were injured there were no fatalities.

Within days after the shooting, Emma Goldman was arrested in Chicago after Czolgosz admitted he was inspired by her to kill the president. Goldman spoke of Czolgosz, explaining, "That boy in Buffalo...committed the act for no personal reasons or gain. He did it for what is his ideal: the good of the people. That is why my sympathies are with him."

Following McKinley's death, the nation followed the proceedings of Leon Czolgosz's trial. He declined legal counsel because, as an anarchist, he did not recognize the right of a court to try him. The court appointed two former New York State Supreme Court justices to represent him. Found guilty, Czolgosz was put to death in the electric chair on the morning of October 29, 1901, at Auburn State Prison in New York, after telling onlookers, "I am not sorry for my crime."

Ida's health steadily declined after her husband's death though her epileptic seizures appeared to stop. She withdrew to the privacy of her home. Relatives looked after her and every day she dressed in black. Although she still suffered from phlebitis and other ailments, Ida made a concerted effort to visit her husband's grave on a regular basis. She died on May 26, 1907. Ida and William McKinley and their two daughters were permanently laid to rest over four months later in the McKinley National Memorial Tomb in Canton.

Theodore Roosevelt, the youngest man ever to become
chief executive of the United States. (*Judge* magazine)

The White House was soon occupied by other tenants as Roosevelt ushered in a new era. (*Frank Leslie's Weekly*)

❧❧❧

CHAPTER XI

REMEMBRANCE AND A LEGACY

William McKinley represented the Victorian Age in America and America in the Victorian Age. Accompanying his deep religious faith was a sense of fatalism. He was a man of sincerity, yet quite humorous. At times formal, he was always courteous.

McKinley loved to meet people and always made them feel he was sensitive to their needs. The twenty-fifth president was certainly one of the friendliest chief executives ever to live in the White House. His patience, integrity and devotion to God and family somehow never interfered with his dedication to the nation.

Some historians have categorized William McKinley as an ineffective leader, a tool of big business, and a president happy to let Congress lead the nation. One recent biographer critically observed, "His reticence was always his great flaw as a leader. With the growth of his importance, he had become increasingly formal and guarded, wary of committing himself on all points except the tariff." None of these conclusions is entirely valid, but McKinley did recognize his strengths and limitations and was not overly concerned with history's judgment. McKinley's philosophy, simplicity, and confidence may be summed up in the credo he expounded: "That's all a man can hope for during his lifetime – to set

In addition to the many thousands of letters of sympathy, Ida received hundreds of official resolutions sent by organizations, institutions and government entities. This one was sent by the United Confederate Veterans in Atlanta. (Stark County Historical Society)

185

an example and, when he is dead, to be an inspiration for history."

McKinley was not a machine politician, nor did he fully comprehend or cultivate the art of public relations. He met and conversed with politicians in public so people could see he was making no deals. He was, in the words of Margaret Leech Pulitzer,"...like a talented artist who needed an impresario, a press agent, and an angel. In Mark Hanna, he found all these." But even Hanna complained that he had very little influence on McKinley's decisions as Ohio governor and president.

As an elected official, McKinley had a deep respect for the public's opinions. The people's diverse and conflicting interests concerned him, and he, as their instrument, sought to correct existing abuses. William McKinley may not have seemed much of a reformer compared to his successor Theodore Roosevelt, but in his own quiet, behind-the-scenes way he fostered and implemented growth. Not concerned with who was credited with success, he was content as long as his goals were achieved. His excessive modesty was a curious trait in a man of such resolute ambition. And as Secretary of State John Hay surmised, "McKinley always got his way."

The lavish attention and gentleness William McKinley gave to his wife were typical of his attitude toward the public as well. He could say 'no' to someone, or refuse a request, and still make him feel he was his friend. One congressman noted that Benjamin Harrison froze people out, Grover Cleveland kicked them out, and McKinley kissed them out.

McKinley possessed a remarkable talent for remembering names, faces, and events. Such a gift was an advantage for a politician. Years

Just one of the many resolutions of condolence. This one was adopted by the Indianapolis Board of Trade. Most of these documents, some very lengthy and elaborately printed and bound, are today in the possession of the McKinley Museum in Canton, Ohio. (Stark County Historical Society)

> *Nature lovers may walk along the McKinley Trail at a small wildlife sanctuary in Poland, Ohio.*

The original site of land before the McKinley Memorial was constructed. (Stark County Historical Society)

Laying of the McKinley Monument cornerstone, November 16, 1905. (Canton *Repository*)

Just a few days after William McKinley died, Ida entered these words into her diary: "I do not want to live if I can't go with my Precious to heaven above where all is love; there will be no sorrowing there."

after he had been introduced to people, he could recall their names upon meeting them again. He often inquired about family members of acquaintances. These abilities firmly secured his support from many people.

Besides remembering names, McKinley often demonstrated his powers of concentration. In spite of the heavy demands and interruptions from his wife and the turmoils of countless political problems, McKinley could focus on a given task, not allowing himself to be sidetracked or dissuaded.

McKinley was also tolerant of others and he had a forgiving nature. He held no grudges. This attribute could be traced to his childhood when schoolmates called him "Fatty." He simply ignored such taunts and forgave his tormentors. Though some may have interpreted this as a sign of weakness, it was in fact one of his strengths.

Other than building a successful law practice and owning some property, the details of business and making money did not appeal to McKinley. Indeed, he was a poor businessman, as evidenced by his embarrassing financial debacle while serving as governor. McKinley once thought he had "struck it rich"

This picture of Ida was taken after the president's death. (Stark County Historical Society)

Workmen laying the granite blocks of the McKinley National Memorial. (Stark County Historical Society)

View of the construction looking from West Nimishillen Creek. (Stark County Historical Society)

Four terraces were carved into Monument Hill to correspond with four landings on the steps. These terraces were dug with horse drawn scoop shovels. (Stark County Historical Society)

Work continued year round on the project. Here, granite blocks were being hauled through the ice and snow. (Stark County Historical Society)

Construction of the reflecting pool, which was drained years later. (Canton *Repository*)

Dedication parade, September 30, 1907. The Marine Band passes the reviewing stand on Canton's public square. (Stark County Historical Society)

when oil was discovered on his small farm near Minerva, Ohio. It yielded only a few barrels, but the farm did provide a chance for him to escape and find some privacy. His strength lay in his abilities as an able administrator who could command more respect than loyalty and delegate authority with positive results.

McKinley never hesitated to maintain order in government or to support effectively those principles of democracy he favored. Under his leadership, the nation became a respected world power, ended a depression, won a war, narrowed the gap of discord between North and South, and planned the construction of the Panama Canal. Perhaps his greatest accomplishments and contributions were best summed up by former President Grover Cleveland: "William McKinley has left us a priceless gift in the example of a useful and pure life, in his fidelity to public trusts and in his demonstration of the value of kindly virtues that not only ennoble but lead to success."

There are many physical reminders of William McKinley. Mount McKinley in central Alaska, at 23,320 feet, is the highest summit in North America. It is located in Denali National Park, formerly established as Mount McKinley National Park in 1917. Statues of McKinley exist in more than a dozen states. Streets, libraries, businesses, veteran organizations, clubs and social groups were named in his honor. Twenty schools in Ohio bear his name.

William McKinley is also associated with two of Ohio's symbols, the state flag and the scarlet carnation. In 1901, the newly-designed, swallow-tailed Ohio banner was flown for the first time at the Pan American Exposition in Buffalo, New York. Its shape resembled the banner carried by Christopher

In his first message to Congress, President Roosevelt announced, "At the time of President McKinley's death he was the most widely loved man in all of the United States; while we have never had any public man of his position who has been so wholly free from the bitter animosities incident to public life...To a standard of lofty integrity in public life he united the tender affections and home virtues which are all-important in the make-up of national character."

President Roosevelt, Canton Mayor Arthur Turnbull and Ohio Governor Andrew Harris at the reviewing stand. (Stark County Historical Society)

Interior of the McKinley National Memorial showing the green granite sarcophagi of William and Ida McKinley. Their two daughters are buried within the surrounding wall. (Stark County Historical Society)

Columbus when he explored America in 1492. Ohio's capital, where McKinley served as governor for two terms, was named in honor of the great explorer.

The scarlet carnation was a McKinley favorite. It was developed in Alliance, Ohio, by Dr. Levi Lamborn, a friend and Democratic candidate for the United States Congress. It soon became a good-luck fetish, and McKinley wore one in his buttonhole in addition to having a fresh supply of them on his office desk each day. Each year on McKinley's birthday, five hundred thirty-five red carnations are distributed to members of the United States House and Senate as a remembrance. Both symbols were officially adopted by the Ohio General Assembly following McKinley's death–the state flag in 1902 and the scarlet carnation in 1904. Today Alliance, Ohio, is known as the "Carnation City" and annually celebrates its contribution as the proud origin of one of the state's symbols.

There were literally thousands of tributes paid to William McKinley. His memory may have faded in the century since his presidency, but as his friend and sometime party opponent Senator Joseph Foraker commented at the time of McKinley's death, "By common consent, he honored the whole human race, and all the race will honor him."

Time will not diminish McKinley's character. It can never erase or undo that which was. John Griggs, McKinley's ex-attorney general said simply, "His pilot stars were Truth and Loyalty." ▨

President Theodore Roosevelt gives the McKinley Natioanl Memorial dedication address, September 30, 1907. (Canton *Repository*)

The McKinley Monument of Canton measures ninety-seven feet high and is made of pink Milford granite from Massachusetts. The interior of the tomb consists of gray marble from Tennessee while the dark green sarcophagi containing the bodies of President and Ida McKinley are of single blocks of granite from Vermont. The sarcophagi rest upon a base of black granite from Wisconsin.

190

A six-inch terra cotta bust of President McKinley. (Private collection of Stewart Witham)

The southern states had seldom been fond of Republican presidents, particularly those of the nineteenth century. William McKinley, however, was an exception. The Age Herald *of Birmingham, Alabama, spoke for most Dixie newspapers when it printed these words following McKinley's death: "The South had good reason to love him, and it will indeed be many a day before a Republican so just will be called to preside over the destinies of the country. The wearers of the gray and the wearers of the blue have united in the week just ended..."*

More than a million school children from around the world contributed money to help build the McKinley National Memorial in Canton. The project was completed in 1907 at a cost of $578,000.

Actual size of memorial medallions. Made of bronze or brass, these commemorative pieces were sold to the public in 1907. (Private collection of Stewart Witham)

The state of Washington preserved this McKinley Stump. (Library of Congress)

The Stark County Historical Society Board of Trustees continues to maintain the McKinley National Memorial. In this picture President Herbert Hoover poses with the McKinley National Memorial Association Trustees, the original caretakers of the memorial. (Canton *Repository*)

The McKinley National Birthplace Memorial in Niles, Ohio. The memorial building houses a complete library and relics of the era of our twenty-fifth president. (McKinley National Birthplace Memorial)

Close-up of the statue at a memorial service in Niles. Helen McKinley, the president's sister, unveiled the statue. (McKinley National Birthplace Memorial)

Stone marker in Buffalo. (Church of The Savior United Methodist of Canton)

A McKinley memorial on the campus of Oberlin College. (Stark County Historical Society)

McKinley statue in San Francisco. (Stark County Historical Society)

Statue of McKinley on the square in Adams, Massachusetts. (Stark County Historical Society)

Sculptor A. Phimister Proctor works on one of the lions which lie at the base of the McKinley Monument in Buffalo, New York. (Stark County Historical Society)

Statues of McKinley were erected in far off cities in Italy and Argentina. This statue was erected outside Philadelphia's City Hall on June 6, 1908. (Stark County Historical Society)

McKinley Monument in Buffalo, dedicated September 5, 1907. (Church of The Savior United Methodist of Canton)

195

Four photos of Mabel McKinley, the president's niece. Although crippled since childhood, Mabel enjoyed a successful career as a singer, earning at one point in her life fifteen hundred dollars a week. (Stark County Historical Society)

Mabel also was a composer, church choir director, and voice teacher. She was the daughter of Abner McKinley. (National McKinley Birthplace Memorial)

The cover of a Mabel McKinley songsheet, found in the McKinley display in Niles. (National McKinley Birthplace Memorial)

In early September of 1900, Mabel married Dr. Herman Baer of Cleveland. The wedding took place in Somerset, Pennsylvania, with the president and first lady in attendance. In 1917 Mabel went to France to entertain troops of the American Expeditionary Force. (Stark County Historical Society)

McKinley paid fourteen thousand dollars cash for this house on North Market Street Canton, Ohio. First used as a hospital after Ida's death, in 1928 a project was approved to move the home to make way for an addition to Mercy Hospital. Part of the house was moved in March of 1929 and the move was completed in July. It was placed in a park on Sixth Street Southwest next to what later became Lincoln High School (today Heritage Christian School). In this picture workmen began moving the house in two sections. (Stark County Historical Society)

During the Great Depression, funds could not be procured to keep the house in proper condition. Eventually it became a health hazard and an eyesore and was torn down. The original site of the home on North Market is now the Stark County District Library. (Canton *Repository*)

Anna McKinley (far right in the front row) sits with her class of students. For more than three decades she served as an educator in Canton. McKinley High School was named in honor of her and her brother William. (Stark County Historical Society)

McKinley is depicted on the $500 Federal Reserve Bank note. (Author's collection)

At least three postage stamps have been issued by the federal government to honor William McKinley. The seven-cent stamp was issued in 1923. The twenty-five-cent stamp came out in 1938 and the most recent one, for twenty-two cents, was issued in 1986. (Author's collection)

The James A. Saxton residence on South Market Street, where the McKinleys lived for a short time was Ida's childhood home. (Stark County Preservation Alliance)

The Saxton House. It has been extensively renovated and houses the offices of the Stark County Foundation and the Education Enhancement Partnership. It is owned by the United States Department of the Interior's National Park Service. A First Ladies Reference Center is located on the first floor. (Stark County Preservation Alliance)

The cargo liner *S.S. President McKinley*, launched August 22, 1967, at Pascagoula, Mississippi. Congressman Frank T. Bow of Ohio (representing the same district McKinley did) dedicated the ship. The five hundred seventy-two foot-long vessel became part of the United States Merchant Marine fleet. (Stark County Historical Society)

ABOUT THE AUTHOR

Rich McElroy has taught social studies and coached athletics at the high school and middle school levels for twenty-seven years. He earned a master's degree from Kent State University took post-graduate courses at the University of Akron. A former city councilman in Canton, Ohio, he remains active in politics. McElroy continues to participate in numerous charitable, athletic, community, and church-related organizations including the Stark County Regional Planning Commission, the Mayor's Literacy Task Force, and several historical societies. He is a lifetime member of the Jaycees and a mason in the McKinley Lodge.

As an authority on baseball and U.S. Presidents, he is busy as a lecturer and guest speaker. He enjoys playing organized baseball and softball, collecting stamps and autographs, oil painting, boating, reading, and teaching. He and his wife Pamela reside in Canton, and have three children and three grandchildren. This is his fifth book.

Tom Hayes

W McKinley

BIBLIOGRAPHY

Adams, James Truslow. *The Epic of America*. Triangle Books, New York, 1931.

Andrews, Byron. *Life and Speeches of William McKinley and Garret A. Hobart*. F. Tennyson Neely, Publishers, Chicago, 1896.

Andrist, Ralph K., editor. *The American Heritage History of the Confident Years*. American Heritage Publishing Company, Inc., New York, 1969.

Anthony, Karl Sferrazza. *First Ladies: Power 1789-1961*, William Morrow and Company, Inc., New York, 1990.

Bailey, Thomas A. *Presidential Greatness*. Appleton-Century, New York, 1966.

Barnard, Harry. *Rutherford B. Hayes And His America*. The Bobbs-Merrill Company, Inc., Indianapolis and New York, 1954.

Barry, Richard H. *The True Story of the Assassination of President McKinley at Buffalo*. Robert Allan Reid, Publisher, Buffalo, New York, 1901.

Basner, Ruth Harpold. *The North Canton Heritage*. Heritage Society of North Canton, Ohio, 1972.

Belden, Henry S. III. *Grand Tour of Ida Saxton McKinley and Sister Mary Saxton Barber 1869*. The Reserve Printing Company, Canton, Ohio, 1985.

Beryl, Frank. *Pictorial History of the Republican Party*. Castle Books, Seacaucus, New Jersey, 1980.

Blodgett, Bonnie and Tice, D.J. *At Home with the Presidents*. The Overlook Press, New York, 1988.

Bow, Frank T. Congressman. *Launching of S.S. President McKinley*. Ingalls Shipbuilding Corporation, Pascagouls, Mississippi, 1967.

Caldwell, H. M. *Bits of Wisdom: William McKinley*. R.H. Woodward Co., New York and Boston, 1901.

Caroli, Betty Boyd. *First Ladies*. Oxford University Press, New York, 1987.

Clark, James Hyde. *The Presidential Battle of 1896*. Globe Bible Publishing Co., Philadelphia, 1896.

Collier, P.F. & Son (editor and publisher), *The Life of William McKinley*. New York, 1901.

Corning, A. Elwood. *William McKinley: A Biographical Study*. Broadway Publishing Co., New York, 1907.

Dawes, Charles G. *The Journal of The McKinley Years*. The Lakeside Press, Chicago, 1950.

DeGregorio, William. *The Complete Book of U.S. Presidents*. Dembner Books, New York, 1984.

Depew, Chauncey M. *My Memoirs of 80 Years*. Charles Scribner's Sons, New York, 1924.

Dunn, Arthur Wallace. *From Harrison to Harding 1888-1921*. G.P. Putnam's Sons, New York, 1922.

Fallows, Samuel. *Life of William McKinley-Our Martyred President*. Regan Printing House, Chicago, 1901.

Frank, Sid and Melick, Arden Davis. *The Presidents: Tidbits and Trivia*. Greenwich House, New York, 1984.

Frassanito, William A. *Antietam: The Photographic Legacy of America's Bloodiest Day*. Charles Scribner's Sons, New York, 1978.

Freidel, Frank. *The Splendid Little War*. Little, Brown and Company, Boston, 1958.

Freidel, Frank and Pencak, William. *The White House: The First Two Hundred Years*. Northeastern University Press, Boston, 1994.

Frost, Elizabeth, editor. *The Bully Pulpit: Quotations From America's Presidents*. New England Publishing Associates, New York, 1988.

Furnas, J.C. *The Americans: A Social History of the United States*. G.P. Putnam's Sons, New York, 1969.

Garrison, Webb. *A Treasury of White House Tales*. Rutledge Hill Press, Nashville, Tennessee, 1989.

Geer, Emily. *First Lady: The Life of Lucy Webb Hayes*. Kent State University Press and The Rutherford B. Hayes Presidential Center, Kent, Ohio, 1984.

Glad, Paul W. *McKinley, Bryan, And The People*. J.B. Lippincott Company, Philadelphia and New York, 1964.

Gould, Lewis L. *The Presidency of William McKinley*. University of Kansas Press, Lawrence, Kansas, 1980.

Grosvenor, Charles H. *William McKinley: His Life And Work*. The Continental Assembly, Washington, D.C., 1901.

Hacker, Louis M. and Kendrick, Benjamin B. *The United States Since 1865*. F. S. Crofts and Co., 1934.

Hay, Peter. *All the Presidents' Ladies*. Viking, New York, 1988.

Heald, Edward Thornton. *The William McKinley Story*. The Stark County Historical Society, Canton, Ohio, 1964.

Higgins, Eva. *William McKinley: An Inspiring Biography*. Daring Publishing Group, Inc., Canton, Ohio, 1989.

Hoover, Irwin Hood (Ike). *Forty-Two Years in the White House*. Houghton Mifflin Company, Boston and New York, 1934.

Hoyt, Edwin P. *William McKinley*. Reilly and Lee Company, Chicago, 1967.

Izant, Grace Goulder. *This Is Ohio*. World Publishing Company, Cleveland and New York, 1953.

Jensen, Amy LaFollette. *The White House And Its Thirty-Two Families*. McGraw-Hill Book Company, New York, 1958.

Jensen, Oliver, Kerr, Joan, and Belsky, Murray. *American Album*. American Heritage Press, New York, 1968.

Johns, A. Wesley. *The Man Who Shot McKinley*. A.S. Barnes and Co., Inc., Cranbury, New Jersey, 1970.

Johnson, Rossiter. *Campfires and Battlefields*. The Civil War Press, New York, 1967.

Josephson, Matthew. *The Politicos: 1865-1896*. Harcourt, Brace and Company, New York, 1938.

Keller, Allan. *The Spanish-American War: A Compact History*. Hawthorn Books, Inc., New York, 1969.

Kirk, Elsie K. *Music at the White House*. A Barra Foundation Book – University of Illinois Press, Urbaba and Chicago, 1986.

Kittler, Glenn D. *Hail to the Chief! The Inauguration Days of Our Presidents*. Hilton Book Company, Philadelphia and New York, 1968.

Kohlsaat, H.H. *From McKinley to Harding*. Charles Scribner's Sons, New York, 1923.

Knepper, George. *An Ohio Portrait*. Ohio Historical Society, Columbus, 1976.

Leech, Margaret. *In the Days of McKinley*. Harper & Brothers, New York, 1959.

Lorant, Stefan. *The Glorious Burden*. Authors Edition, Inc., Lenox, Massachusetts, 1976.

McElroy, Richard L. *American Presidents*. Daring Books, Canton, Ohio, 1984.

McElroy Richard L. *American Presidents, Volume II*. Daring Books, Canton, Ohio, 1989.

McElroy, Richard L. *James A. Garfield - His Life and Times: A Pictorial History*. Daring Books, Canton, Ohio, 1986.

McKinley National Memorial Association. *The Nation's Memorial to William McKinley*. Canton, Ohio, 1913.

Mead, William B. and Dickson, Paul. *Baseball: The Presidents' Game*. Farragut Publishing Company, Washington, D.C., 1993.

Melder, Keith. *Hail to the Candidate*. Smithsonian Institution Press, Washington, D.C., 1992.

Morgan, H. Wayne. *William McKinley and His America*. Syracuse University Press, Syracuse, New York, 1963.

Morris, Charles and Ellis, Edward S. *Great Issues and National Leaders*. W. F. Scull, Washington, D.C., 1901.

Morris, Edmund. *The Rise of Theodore Roosevelt*. Coward, McCann & Geoghegan, Inc., New York, 1979.

Moses, John B. and Cross, Wilbur. *Presidential Courage*. W.W. Norton and Company, New York, 1980.

Olcott, Charles S. *The Life of William McKinley*. Houghton Mifflin Company, Boston and New York, 1916.

Opper, Frederick B. *Willie and Papa*. Grosset & Dunlap, New York, 1901.

O'Toole, G.J.A. *The Spanish War: An American Epic*. W.W. Norton & Company, New York, 1984.

Porter, Robert P. *The Life of William McKinley-Soldier, Lawyer, Statesman*. The N. G. Hamilton Publishing Co., Cleveland, Ohio, 1896.

Prescott, Lawrence F. *1896-The Great Campaign*. Loyal Publishing Co., Washington, D.C., 1896.

Ramsayer, Ralph K. *History of Christ United Presbyterian Church: 150th Anniversary*. Consolidated Graphic Art Corporation, Canton, Ohio, 1971.

Rhodes, James Ford. *The McKinley And Roosevelt Administrations 1897-1909*, McMillan Company, New York, 1922.

Sandler, Martin. *This Was America*. Media Enterprises, Inc. and Little, Brown, & Company, Boston, 1980.

Siedel, Frank. *Out of the Midwest*. World Publishing Company, Cleveland, 1953.

Sievers, Harry J. *Benjamin Harrison-Hoosier President*. The Bobbs-Merrill Company, Inc., Indianapolis, Indiana, 1968.

Simpson, Jeffery. *The Way Life Was*. Praeger Publishers, New York and Washington, 1974.

Singleton, Esther. *The Story of The White House, Vol. II*. The McClure Company, New York, 1907.

Smith, Ernest Ashton. *Allegheny—A Century of Education, 1815-1915*. The Allegheny College History Company, Meadeville, Pennsylvania, 1916.

Smith, Page. *The Rise of Industrial America*. McGraw-Hill Book Company, New York, 1984.

Snow, Jane Elliott. *The Life of William McKinley*. Imperial Press – Gardner Printing Company, Cleveland, Ohio, 1908.

Spielman, William Carl. *William McKinley – Stalwart Republican*, Exposition Press, New York, 1954.

Stealey, O.O. *Twenty Years in the Press Gallery*. Publishers Printing Company, New York, 1906.

Stille, Samuel Harden. *Ohio Builds A Nation*. Arlendale Book House, Chicago and New York City, 1941.

Sullivan, Mark. *Our Times: 1900-1925*. Charles Scribner's Sons, New York, 1971.

Tonner, A.C. *Illustrated Industrial Canton*. The Repository Printing Co., Canton, Ohio, 1896.

Townsend, Col. G.W. *Memorial Life of William McKinley -Our Martyred President*. Memorial Publishing Company, Philadelphia, 1901.

Van Tassel, Charles Sumner. *The Book of Ohio*. C. S. Van Tassell, Publisher, Columbus and Toledo, 1901.

Werstein, Irving. *1898: The Spanish-American War*. Cooper Square Publishers, Inc., New York, 1966.

Willets, Gilson. *Inside History of The White House*. The Christian Herald, New York, 1908.

Williams, T. Harry. *Hayes of the Twenty-third*. Alfred A. Knopf, Inc., New York, 1965.

Williams, H. Z. *History of Trumbull and Mahoning Counties*. H. Z. Williams and Bro., Cleveland, Ohio, 1882.

Wright, Marcus, General. *Wright's Official History of The Spanish-American War*. War Records Office, Washington, D.C., 1900.

The following magazines were also used: *American Heritage, Judge, Puck, Ohio Cues, Frank Leslie's Weekly, The Smithsonian, Harpers, Harper's Weekly, Ohioana Quarterly, Colliers, Mankind* and *The Buckeye Flyer*.

INDEX

Los Angeles, CA 57, 103, 149
Luks, George 75
Luzon 125
Lynch, William 24, 26
Lyon, France 35

M

MacKenzie, Grace 164
Mackinac Island, MI 67
Maddock, John 65
Maine, U.S.S. 108-111, 127, 128
Malloy, Thomas 68
Manchu rulers 126
Manifest Destiny 126
Manila, Philippines 118, 124
Mann, Dr. Matthew 162, 165
Marconi, Guglielmo 131
Martinsburg, WV 22
Masons (Masonic Lodge) 24
Massachusetts 190
Massillon, OH 28, 37, 67, 96
May, Mary McKinley. *See* McKinley, Mary
McClane, Eleanor 3
McClellan, George 14
McClymond, Edna 96
McGuffey, William Holmes 131
McKenna, Joseph 84, 85
McKinlay, James 1
McKinley
  (sister-Mary May) 6
  Abigail 7
  Abner 7, 47, 49, 72, 100, 153, 163, 196
  Anna (sister) 6, 7, 23, 43, 51, 198
  Annie (sister-in-law) 7
  David (brother) 6, 37
  David (great grandfather) 3
  David (great-great-great-grandfather) 1
  Eleanor McClane 3
  Esther 1
  Grace 51, 96
  Helen 6, 7, 23, 43
  Hope 6
  Ida 47
  Ida (daughter) 28
  James (brother) 6
  James F. (nephew) 38, 114
  James, Jr 51, 114, 115
  James S. (grandfather) 3
  John 1
  Katherine (Katie) 28, 48, 49
  Mabel 7, 196
  Margaret 1
  Mary (sister-Mary May) 6
  Mary Rose (grandmother) 3
  Nancy Allison 6, 72-75
  Sarah Duncan 6
  Sarah Gray 3
  William Sr 6
McKinley Clubs 67

McKinley, President S.S. 199
McKinley Quartet 68
McKinley Senior High School (Canton, OH) 198
Meadville, PA 10
Media, PA 43
Mercer County, PA 3
Mercy Hospital 197
Merritt, Wesley 117
Mexican War 7
Meyers Lake (Canton, OH) 26, 158
Michigan 100
Milburn, John 155, 162, 163, 165
Miles, Nelson A. 119
Minerva, OH 68, 93, 189
Minneapolis, MN 38
Mississippi 88, 100, 133
Missouri 69
Monroe Doctrine 107
Montauk Point, NY 114
Morton, Levi 60, 61, 69
Mosquito Creek, OH 7
Mount Holyoke College, MA 96
Mount McKinley National Park 189
Mt. Union College, OH 26, 86, 141
Mynter, Dr. Herman 162, 165

N

Navarre, OH 24, 129
Nebraska 117
Nevada 34
New Castle, PA 6
New Jersey 66
New Orleans, LA 146
New York City, NY 48, 61, 72, 78, 105, 112, 135, 145
Niagara Falls, NY 153, 154
Niles, OH 7, 67, 129, 193
North Canton, OH (New Berlin) 23
North Carolina 87, 143
Nowak Saloon 159

O

Oakland, CA 104, 150, 152
Oberlin College, OH 194
Ohio Society 105
Ohio, U.S.S. 104
Olympia, U.S.S. 118
Open Door policy 86, 126, 134
Opiquan, battle of. *See* Winchester
Opper, Frederick 80
Oquendo 121
Oregon 72
Oregon, U.S.S. 116
Osborne, Will 11, 26, 67

P

Pan American Exposition 151, 152, 157, 162, 189

Panama Canal 85, 189
Panic of 1857 10
Panic of 1893 36
Paris 116
Park, Dr. Roswell 162, 164, 165
Parker, John 159, 161
Pascagoula, MS 199
Paulus Hook, battle of 3
Pauncefote, Lord Julian 92
Pausch, E. L. 168
Peking, China (Beijing) 126
Pendleton Act 87
Pennsylvania 86, 87, 114
Philadelphia, PA 65, 172
Philippine Insurrection 116, 117, 119, 124, 125
Philippines 86, 107, 108, 116, 117, 119
Phoenix, AZ 147
Platt, Thomas 60, 61
Plunkett family 145
Poland, OH 6, 7, 10, 11, 186
Poland Seminary 9
Pope Pius IX 47
Porter, Addison 85
Porter, Horace 144
Portland, ME 130
Pro Football Hall of Fame 24
Proctor, A. Phimister 195
Pueblo, CO 55
Puerto Rico 116
Pughe, J.S. 61
Pulitzer, Joseph 66, 109
Pulitzer, Margaret Leech 186

Q

Quay, Matthew 61, 69
Queen Victoria 151
Quincy, IL 95

R

Ravenna, OH 84, 175
Rebecca Iron Furnace 3
Reconstruction Era 129
Red Cloud, Chief 163
Reed, Billy 68
Reed, Thomas 34, 61
Republican National Committee 61, 67
Republican National Convention
  1892 38
  1896 60
  1900 77, 78
Rixey. Dr. Presley 152, 162, 164
Röentgen, Wilhelm C. 131
Roosevelt, Theodore 58, 61, 77-79, 84, 85, 104, 116, 120, 151, 164, 169, 174, 184, 186, 190
Root, Elihu 86, 87, 96
Rose, Andrew 3